THE BIRDWATCHER'S DICTIONARY

The Campbell's
Foan hill. N. Dysart
Fife
July 1996

THE BIRDWATCHER'S DICTIONARY

by Peter Weaver

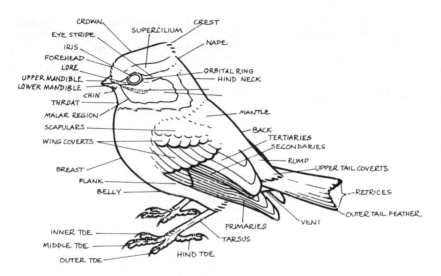

With drawings by
MICHAEL HODGSON

T & A D POYSER
Calton

© Peter Weaver 1981

ISBN 0 85661 028 3

First published in 1981 by T & A D Poyser Ltd
Town Head House, Calton, Waterhouses, Staffordshire, England

Text set in 9/10pt Linotron Plantin, printed and bound in Great Britain at The Pitman Press, Bath

Introduction

A scientist might call it an oviparous vertebrate. It could be a lifer for a twitcher, or a control for a ringer. It might be drumming or jugging, in a trip or a wisp. You could split it, dip out on it, or even cause it to explode. It is, of course, a bird.

Birdwatchers' language is a mixture of science and slang. You might well hear nictitating membrane and marsh cowboy mentioned in almost the same breath. If you read about or talk about birds you are bound to meet expressions like these, but discovering their precise meanings can be remarkably difficult. With the number of birdwatchers increasing rapidly there is more than ever a need for a book about birds and words.

The aim of this book is to assemble in one place definitions of those terms and phrases which are most likely to be encountered by birdwatchers in Britain. The dictionary is intended both for beginners and for the more experienced. Those developing an interest in birds come across many terms with meanings unknown to them, while even expert ornithologists may be vague about the precise definition of an expression which they often meet and sometimes use.

The entries have been made as brief and as simple as is reasonable for adequate explanations of meanings. They are basically definitions, because the book is intended as a dictionary rather than an encyclopaedia, but a little meat has frequently been added to the bare bones, either because it is necessary for a true understanding of a particular term or because I have tried to encourage the curiosity which can so greatly increase enjoyment of an interest such as birdwatching. Besides, I hope that browsers, as well as those looking for a particular definition, will turn the pages.

WHAT IS IN THE BOOK

There are two sections, the dictionary and the appendices, the latter forming a short supplement. The dictionary consists of an alphabetical list of terms with their definitions. The selection of the entries has, unavoidably, been subjective, but in making my choice I have been able to draw upon my experience as a birdwatcher and teacher of ornithology. Nevertheless, there are bound to be inclusions and omissions which will seem unjustified to some readers, and for such I apologise.

The content of the dictionary includes the following categories:

1   Scientific terms (such as loop migration and natural selection).

2   Birdwatchers' slang (such as gardening and ringtail).

3   British names of birds where it may not be obvious which group or species is implied – for example, the sometimes indeterminate group names (such as seabird), the names of subspecies (such as Black-bellied Dipper),

5

the names of plumage phases (such as Bridled Guillemot) and alternative names for species (such as Hedge Sparrow).

4   Names of organisations, projects, etc (such as Hawk Trust and Nest Record Scheme).

Omissions from the dictionary include the following:

1   Terms unlikely to be encountered by the birdwatcher in Britain (such highly specialised terms as chalaza—part of the internal structure of an egg), and those terms used only abroad (such as whistler, North American slang for the Goldeneye).

2   Expressions with obvious meanings (such as eggshell and eyelid).

3   Material included in the appendices (with a few exceptions).

4   Regional bird names, unless they can be regarded as alternative names likely to be encountered by birdwatchers.

LOOKING UP ENTRIES

The headings in the dictionary are arranged in alphabetical order of their initial letters. Where an expression consists of more than one word, the order of the words is not changed (French Partridge does not appear as Partridge, French).

Words placed within parentheses ( ) in the heading may or may not be part of the term or expression in normal usage.

Many entries are explained in the course of defining other terms and, to avoid frequent repetition, there are many cross-references, which I hope will not be found too irritating.

Words printed in small capital letters within a definition are themselves the subject of a separate heading and definition.

A NOTE ON BIRD NAMES

As explained above, the dictionary section includes only those bird names likely to cause confusion. 'Standard' vernacular names of birds on the British and Irish List are given, with their scientific names, in Appendix D.

The dictionary follows ornithological convention by giving capital initial letters to names of species, as in Chaffinch, but not to group names, such as finch. This practice avoids confusion, making it clear, for example, that Swallow refers to a particular species (*the* Swallow *Hirundo rustica*), whereas swallow, without a capital initial letter, refers to any member of the swallow family.

Scientific names, in accordance with worldwide usage, are printed in italic type where they refer to genera or species. The generic names are given capital initial letters (as are the names of orders and families), unlike the specific (or subspecific) names – for example, *Parus caeruleus* (Blue Tit). Subsequent mention of the generic name within an entry is abbreviated to the initial letter, so that the scientific names for Blue Tit and Great Tit, if appearing in the same entry, would be given as *Parus caeruleus* and *P. major*. The use of scientific names is fully explained in the relevant entries in the dictionary.

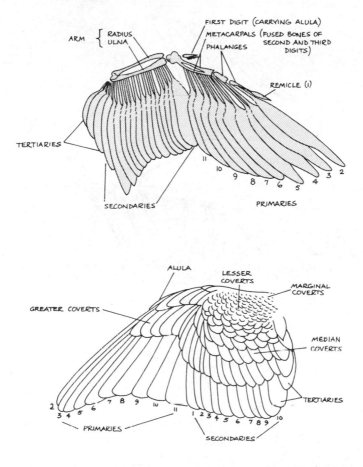

Wing structure and feathering of a typical bird

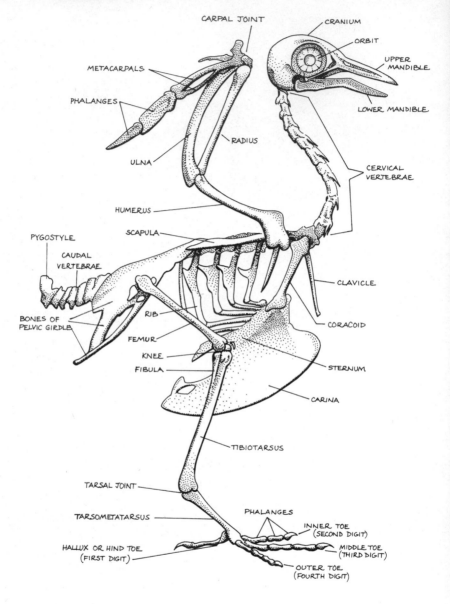

General skeleton of a typical bird

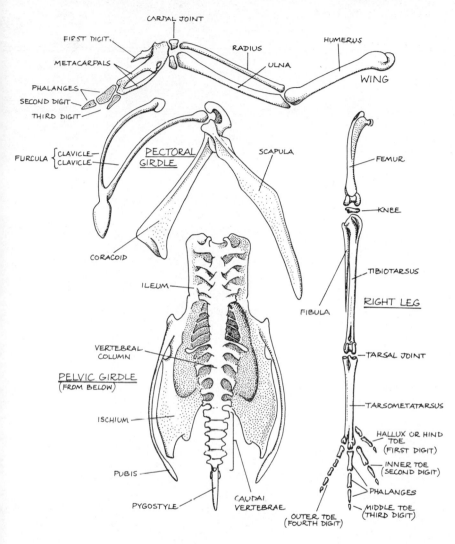

Pelvic and pectoral girdles and limbs of a typical bird

Abdomen   The rear section of the body, containing the REPRODUCTIVE SYSTEM and the major part of the ALIMENTARY SYSTEM. The other body divisions are the head and the THORAX.

Aberrant   Abnormal or unusual. An aberrant individual is one which in some way is not typical of its SPECIES, for example one showing features of ALBINISM. The Long-tailed Tit *Aegithalos caudatus* can be described as aberrant from the 'true' tits (FAMILY Paridae), so much so that it is placed in a separate family (Aegithalidae).

Abmigration   Movement of an individual from one breeding area to another by pairing in a winter flock with a bird from the new area and travelling there with it on spring MIGRATION.   Examples of abmigrants are found in bird groups whose winter flocks contain birds from various breeding grounds mixed together, notably ducks (FAMILY Anatidae).

Abrasion   Wear of the feathers. In cases where the tips are coloured differently from the lower parts of the feathers, abrasion can change the appearance of the PLUMAGE quite considerably, and in this way winter plumage can become breeding plumage without the necessity for MOULT. This 'abrasive moult' is found in many PASSERINE birds, for example the Starling *Sturnus vulgaris* and the Chaffinch *Fringilla coelebs*.

Accentor   A member of the FAMILY Prunellidae, of which by far the most widespread is the Dunnock *Prunella modularis*. This family of 13 SPECIES is the only bird family which is confined to the PALEARCTIC (REGION).

Accidental (species)   See VAGRANT.

ACCIPITER : SPARROWHAWK

Accipiter   The SCIENTIFIC NAME of a GENUS of the FAMILY Accipitridae, often used as a vernacular name for the birds concerned, which are also called 'bird hawks' after their main prey. The most common accipiter in the British Isles is the Sparrowhawk *A. nisus*.

Acclimatisation   The INTRODUCTION of a SPECIES to an area to which it is not native by gradually accustoming individuals to the climate, offering food and shelter where necessary, until a truly self-supporting POPULATION has developed.

Acro　A member of the GENUS *Acrocephalus*, part of the FAMILY Sylviidae. This abbreviation for the SCIENTIFIC NAME of the genus is used mainly in RINGING and TWITCHING. Among the SPECIES concerned are the Sedge Warbler *A. schoenobaenus* and the Reed Warbler *A. scirpaceus.*

Active anting　See ANTING.

Adaptation　Development of characteristics to fit the ENVIRONMENT. As part of the process of EVOLUTION, adaptation proceeds by MUTATION and is closely linked with NATURAL SELECTION. It may lead to ADAPTIVE RADIATION and to CONVERGENCE.

Adaptive radiation　The EVOLUTION of two or more distinct SPECIES from a single original stock, each of the new species being adapted to a different ENVIRONMENT.

Addled　Failing to hatch.

Adult　An individual which has reached the stage in its life beyond which it no longer changes physically with age, in contrast to a JUVENILE or an IMMATURE.

Adventitious coloration　Superficial staining on the body. For example, the heads and necks of swans (GENUS *Cygnus*) may be stained a rusty colour by iron in the water.

Advertising display　A type of BEHAVIOUR employed to attract a mate, such a DISPLAY usually being accompanied by some kind of SONG.

Aerial feeder　A bird which obtains most or all of its food in flight. Although some types of RAPTOR feed in this way, the term normally refers to those birds which spend their time HAWKING insects, namely the nightjars (FAMILY Caprimulgidae), the swifts (family Apodidae), the swallows (family Hirundinidae) and the flycatchers (family Muscicapidae).

Aerie　See EYRIE.

Afrotropical (Region)　See ZOOGEOGRAPHICAL REGION.

Aftershaft　A small feather which is an offshoot of a larger one.

Agonistic display　See ANTAGONISTIC DISPLAY.

Aigrette　A loose, elongated 'ornamental' PLUME, seen, for example, on the BACK of the Grey Heron *Ardea cinerea.*

Air sac　A cavity in a bird's body connected to the lungs, and so part of the RESPIRATORY SYSTEM. Birds have at least five air sacs, which increase breathing efficiency and reduce weight, each of these functions being an aid to flying.

Air speed   The rate of progress of a bird in relation to the air in which it is flying. The bird's speed in relation to the ground ('ground speed') will vary according to the wind, in that it will consist of its air speed plus or minus the wind speed (depending on whether the bird is flying wholly or partly against or with the wind). Therefore, a bird with an air speed of 20 kph flying into a head wind of 12 kph will have a ground speed of 8 kph.

Alar   Of the wing.

Albinism   Lack of pigment on the body, so that a full albino has white feathers and pink eyes. A partially albinistic bird, with white patches in its PLUMAGE, is said to be 'leucistic', although this term is also used to describe very pale individuals which might also be called 'dilute albinos'. Those birds which are normally white are not albinos, and do not have pink eyes, albinism being an ABERRANT condition.

Albumen   The 'white' of the egg, being a protein store (like the yolk) for the developing EMBRYO.

Alexander Library   The largest collection of modern ornithological literature in the British Isles, housed at the EDWARD GREY INSTITUTE in Oxford, and named after the Institute's first director, W. B. Alexander. The library was established in 1938 and contains journals, offprints and manuscripts as well as books. Members of the BRITISH ORNITHOLOGISTS' UNION and the BRITISH TRUST FOR ORNITHOLOGY are entitled to use its facilities.

Alimentary system   Basically a long tube, called the 'gut' or 'alimentary canal', along which food passes and is gradually digested. The gut begins at the mouth and its main sections are the OESOPHAGUS (with or without a CROP), the GIZZARD and the INTESTINE, ending at the CLOACA. Included in the alimentary system are the liver (which produces bile among other functions) and the pancreas (which produces digestive juices and insulin).

Allen's Rule   The contention that within an animal SPECIES the extremities of the body tend to be longer in the warmer regions of its DISTRIBUTION and shorter in the cooler regions.

Allopatric   See SYMPATRIC.

Allopreening   The PREENING of one individual by another, best seen during COURTSHIP in certain bird groups, notably the crows (FAMILY Corvidae).

Alternate plumage   See BASIC PLUMAGE.

Altitudinal migration   Movement of highland birds down to lower levels for the winter and back to higher altitudes for the BREEDING SEASON, the birds concerned not being involved in MIGRATION in the usual sense. The Red Grouse *Lagopus lagopus* and the Dipper *Cinclus cinclus* provide examples.

Altricial See NIDICOLOUS.

Alula A structure consisting of four small feathers growing on a bird's 'thumb', also known as the 'bastard wing'. It controls the airflow over the leading edge of the wing.

Ambivalence A type of BEHAVIOUR resulting from the clash of two opposing motivations, such as aggression and fear. Ambivalence is well seen in encounters between neighbouring TERRITORY holders, with each bird alternately attacking and retreating.

American blackbird See ICTERID (BLACKBIRD).

American oriole See ICTERID (BLACKBIRD).

American sparrow See NEW WORLD SPARROW.

American warbler See NEW WORLD WARBLER.

Anatomy The study of the bodily structure of animals. The study of the functioning of the body is called 'physiology'.

Angel See RADAR ORNITHOLOGY.

Antagonistic display A type of behaviour involving aggression, such a DISPLAY being well seen in the defence of TERRITORY. It may also be called 'agonistic display'.

Anterior Towards the front. The converse, 'posterior,' means towards the back.

Anthropomorphism The practice of ascribing human qualities to animals other than man.

Anting Placing ants among the feathers ('active anting') or simply allowing ants to run through the PLUMAGE ('passive anting'). Like DUSTING and SMOKE BATHING, anting presumably discourages ECTOPARASITE infestation.

Anus See CLOACA.

Anvil A stone or other hard object on which a Song Thrush *Turdus philomelos* smashes the shells of snails so that the soft inside parts can be eaten. Anvils can be easily identified by the litter of shell fragments around them.

Appendage A projection from the body, such as a limb or a CREST.

Appetitive behaviour A type of activity which has a definite goal, such as nest building, although a bird may not actually be 'aware' of the end product towards which it is striving.

Aquatic Living in or on water. Most aquatic birds show some kind of ADAPTATION to their ENVIRONMENT, notably lobing or webbing of the feet, as found respectively in the grebes (FAMILY Podicipedidae) and the gulls (family Laridae). In addition to the truly aquatic (swimming) birds, there are many RIPARIAN types.

Aquiline   Of eagles (FAMILY Accipitridae), or 'eagle-like'.

Arboreal   Connected with trees.

Arena   See LEK.

Arm   The section of the wing between the body and the CARPAL JOINT, the rest of the wing constituting the HAND. The bones of the arm are the HUMERUS, RADIUS and 'ulna'. The SECONDARY and TERTIARY feathers are carried on the arm.

Arrested moult   The situation where the progress of a bird's MOULT is suspended for a period, to be resumed later. An example of a SPECIES which normally arrests its moult is the Common Tern *Sterna hirundo*, which begins its moult prior to the autumn MIGRATION, suspends it during the migration itself and then continues to moult after arrival in its winter quarters.

Ascendant moult   See DESCENDANT MOULT.

Aspect   The compass direction in which a piece of land faces. Mention of aspect is an important component of descriptions of HABITAT, especially with regard to a NEST SITE.

Aspergillosis   A fungal disease particularly affecting the RESPIRATORY SYSTEM, and found especially in WILDFOWL and GALLINACEOUS birds.

Asynchronous hatching   The situation in which all the eggs in a CLUTCH do not hatch at (more or less) the same time, as is more usual among birds, but have their hatching spread over several days. It is well seen in the various types of RAPTOR, and is an ADAPTATION to a type of food supply which may fluctuate. During seasons when food is short the later hatched young will probably starve as the earlier hatched young, being larger and stronger, deprive them of food, and so the size of the BROOD is reduced to a level in balance with the available food supply. In years of plenty all the young may be able to survive. In 'synchronous hatching' all the eggs hatch at more or less the same time.

Atlassing   Collection of data for use in compiling an atlas showing the DISTRIBUTION of birds in the area concerned. Since the pioneering work of the BRITISH TRUST FOR ORNITHOLOGY and the IRISH WILDBIRD CONSERVANCY in 1968–72 (resulting in *The Atlas of Breeding Birds in Britain and Ireland*), several European countries have produced breeding bird atlases. The European Ornithological Atlas Committee, formed in 1971, co-ordinates these activities. (*See overleaf*).

Atrophy   Reduction in size of an ORGAN as a result of lack of use. In the course of EVOLUTION, for example, the legs and feet of swifts (FAMILY Apodidae) have become atrophied as their lifestyle has become more aerial.

The Balearic subspecies is a regular autumn visitor to the English Channel.

Banding   The North American term for RINGING.

Banger   A Swift *Apus apus* which strikes the entrance to a nest chamber by touching it with its wings and then flies off without landing. A banger appears not to strike its own nest entrance, and the significance of this BEHAVIOUR, which may involve more than one bird and more than one nest, is not known.

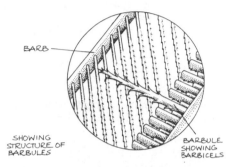

SHOWING STRUCTURE OF BARBULES

BARB

BARBULE SHOWING BARBICELS

Barb   A horizontal branch from the shaft (RACHIS) of a feather, also called a 'ramus'. It carries the 'barbules' which are so arranged that those on one barb interlock with those of its neighbours, being held by tiny hooks called 'barbicels' or 'hamuli'. With this arrangement a bird has only to run its bill along a disarrayed feather while PREENING to return it to its proper neatness. The barbs taken all together make up the 'vane' or 'web' of the feather.

Barbicel   See BARB.

Barbule   See BARB.

Bare parts   The areas of the body surface which are not covered by feathers, namely the bill, eyes, legs and feet, together with any unfeathered skin. They were formerly, and inappropriately, called the 'soft parts'.

Barred Woodpecker   An alternative name for the Lesser Spotted Woodpecker *Dendrocopos minor*.

Basic plumage   A North American term for the 'non-breeding' PLUMAGE of a SPECIES which has a special breeding plumage, and for the normal year-round plumage of a species which does not. In the first case, the special breeding plumage is called 'alternate', and if a third plumage stage exists, this is called 'supplementary'.

Bastard wing   See ALULA.

Bay duck See SEA DUCK.

Beached Bird Survey An international regular count of bird corpses washed up on the coast. It involves those countries bordering on the North Sea, the Irish Sea and the English Channel, and forms a useful monitoring system for bird MORTALITY at sea, especially that caused by OILING. The survey, which originated in Britain in 1965, is jointly organised by the ROYAL SOCIETY FOR THE PROTECTION OF BIRDS and the SEABIRD GROUP.

Bearded Reedling An alternative name for the Bearded Tit *Panurus biarmicus*, which is now considered to be unrelated to the 'true' tits (FAMILY Paridae) and is placed in the babbler family (Timaliidae).

Behaviour Habits and activities, usually divided into 'breeding behaviour', 'feeding behaviour' and so on. The study of animal behaviour ('ethology'), apart from its intrinsic interest, throws light on various aspects of ZOOLOGY, including PHYSIOLOGY and TAXONOMY.

Belly The lowest part of the undersurface of a bird.

Belt transect See TRANSECT.

Bergmann's Rule The contention that individuals of a warm-blooded animal SPECIES increase in size the further from the Equator they occur. This is perhaps an ADAPTATION to reduce heat loss, as large animals lose heat more slowly than small ones.

Bill-clappering, bill-clattering or **bill-fencing** The members of a pair clashing their bills together, producing a sometimes far-carrying sound. It is a form of DISPLAY characteristic of the Grey Heron *Ardea cinerea* at the nest.

Billing The members of a pair gently touching bills or caressing with their bills, also called 'nebbing'. It is well seen in the pigeons (FAMILY Columbidae).

Binding-to Fastening on to prey by a RAPTOR in mid-air, often at the end of a STOOP. This term is one of several which ornithologists have borrowed from FALCONRY.

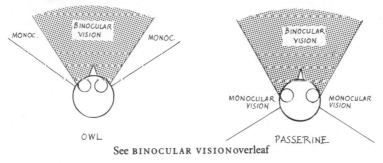

See BINOCULAR VISION overleaf

Binocular vision The situation where the fields of view of the eyes overlap, as opposed to 'monocular vision', in which such overlap does not occur. In most types of birds binocular vision is limited, the most notable exceptions being the owls (ORDER Strigiformes). Binocular vision assists in the pinpointing of objects, and so is useful to the latter birds for catching prey, but for most types wide visibility is more important and so monocular vision is better developed.

Binomi(n)al nomenclature The internationally agreed and universally accepted system of naming SPECIES. It was invented by LINNAEUS and consists of the application of a double SCIENTIFIC NAME to each species. The first name (the 'generic name') indicates the GENUS to which the species belongs and always has a capital initial. It is usually abbreviated to this letter after its first mention in a passage of text. The second name (the 'specific name') identifies the species itself and always has a small initial. Thus the scientific name of the Blue Tit is *Parus caeruleus*, while that of the Great Tit, which is placed in the same genus, is *P. major*. The same specific name may occur in more than one genus: for example, the Great Spotted Woodpecker has the scientific name *Dendrocopos major*. Also a species might have its generic and specific names the same, as in the Magpie *Pica pica*. Each combination, however, is unique. For naming SUBSPECIES the system of TRINOMIAL NOMENCLATURE is used.

Biological clock See ORIENTATION.

Biological Records Centre See NATURAL ENVIRONMENT RESEARCH COUNCIL.

Biology The academic study of the living ORGANISM in both its general and particular aspects. Biology is basically divided into 'botany' (the study of plants) and ZOOLOGY (the study of animals), but has various more generalised divisions, such as ECOLOGY, PHYSIOLOGY and TAXONOMY.

Biomass The weight of living matter. For a particular place where its estimation has been possible, a figure may be quoted for the bird biomass, and it may be expressed as a percentage of the total animal biomass. Likewise, figures for individual SPECIES can be related to the total bird biomass. Such data may be more useful than percentages based on POPULATION, as biomass takes into account differences in the sizes of the various species.

Biome A major vegetation region of the world, for example the TUNDRA or the BOREAL FOREST. Each biome has a characteristic AVIFAUNA.

Biometric Concerned with the accurate measurement of the characteristics of living things ('biometry'), such as dimensions and weights.

Biotic Concerned with the living part of the ENVIRONMENT, as opposed to the non-living physical part.

Biotope See HABITAT.

Bipedal   Two-legged (literally 'two-footed').

Birder   See TWITCHING.

Bird fancier   See AVICULTURE.

Bird gardening   The practice of attempting to attract an increased number and variety of birds to a garden, by providing food, water, shelter and nesting places, by such means as the introduction of bird tables and nestboxes and the planting of suitable shrubs.

Bird hawk   See ACCIPITER.

Bird lime   A sticky substance (made from bark) smeared on twigs to catch small birds by their feet. This practice is illegal in the British Isles under the bird PROTECTION LAWS.

Bird Observatories Council   An organisation founded in 1970 (replacing the former Bird Observatories Committee) with the object of promoting a national BIRD OBSERVATORY network and coordinating the activities of the various independent observatories.

Bird observatory   A station established mainly for the study of bird MIGRATION, particularly by means of RINGING. The bird observatories of the British Isles are situated at key points on migration routes, all of them being on coasts or small islands. The fourteen which are affiliated to the BIRD OBSERVATORIES COUNCIL are shown on the map overleaf.

Bird of prey   See RAPTOR.

Bird Protection Acts   See PROTECTION LAWS.

Bird recorder   A person appointed by a local ornithological society to keep records of birds seen in its area. The recorder may also be the editor of the local BIRD REPORT. In the case of RARITY records, they are submitted by the recorder to a RARITIES COMMITTEE.

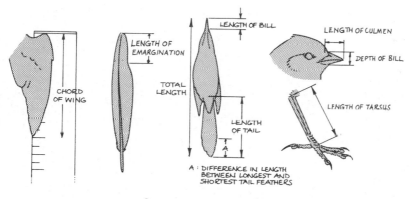

See BIOMETRIC, opposite

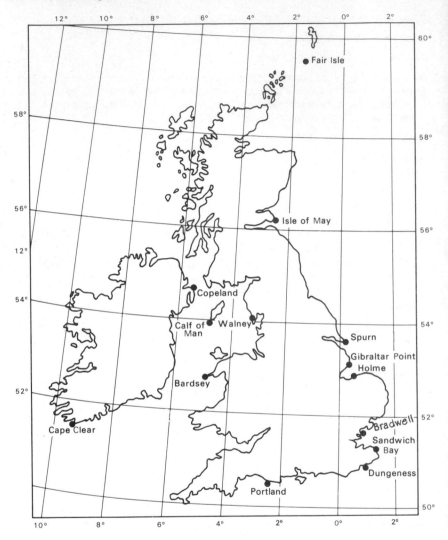

Bird observatories in Britain and Ireland – see entry, previous page

Bird Report   A publication which summarises observations of birds in a particular area over a particular period. Most such reports are published annually by local ornithological societies and in England and Wales they refer mainly to counties. Such a report contains a SYSTEMATIC LIST of bird records and may include papers or articles on topics of local interest.

Bird sanctuary An officially designated and defined area in which all birds, their nests and their eggs and young are fully protected. The Secretary of State for the Environment has the power to establish such sanctuaries by applying 'sanctuary orders' under the bird PROTECTION LAWS. Unofficially, any place where some measure of protection is given to birds may be called a bird sanctuary.

Bird strike A collision between an aircraft and a bird or a group of birds, most frequently occurring at coastal airfields where large numbers of gulls (FAMILY Laridae) congregate.

Birdwatcher's Code of Conduct A code of practice devised by consultation between the leading British ornithological organisations, and first published in 1980 by the ROYAL SOCIETY FOR THE PROTECTION OF BIRDS. It is summarised in Appendix C of this book.

Black-bellied Dipper A continental SUBSPECIES of the Dipper *Cinclus cinclus*, examples of which arrive irregularly in eastern Britain in winter. The race concerned, *C.c. cinclus*, breeds mainly in northern Europe.

Blackcock See BLACK GAME.

Black Game A general name for the Black Grouse *Tetrao tetrix*, the males of which are known as 'blackcocks' and the females as 'greyhens'.

Black goose A member of the GENUS *Branta*, part of the FAMILY Anatidae, for example the Barnacle Goose *B. leucopsis*.

Black Scoter An alternative name for the Common Scoter *Melanitta nigra*.

Blade See WEB.

Bleating See DRUMMING.

Blind See HIDE.

Blue Fulmar A colour phase of the Fulmar *Fulmarus glacialis* in which the white PLUMAGE is replaced by grey. It is not regarded as a SUBSPECIES, but merely as an example of DIMORPHISM. Few British Fulmars are blue, but the phase may dominate in an Arctic POPULATION.

Blue Goose See LESSER SNOW GOOSE.

Blue-headed Wagtail A continental European SUBSPECIES of the Yellow Wagtail *Motacilla flava*. It has the SCIENTIFIC NAME *M.f. flava*, the British breeding subspecies being *M.f. flavissima*. The blue-headed subspecies has been recorded breeding in small numbers in Britain, mainly in south-east England.

Body cavity A space within an animal's body, usually named after the type of ORGAN which it contains, for example the 'pericardial cavity' around the heart and the 'pleural cavities' containing the lungs.

Bog See MARSH.

Bonxie An alternative name for the Great Skua *Stercorarius skua*, originating in Shetland and now widely used.

Boom   A far-carrying vocal sound produced by the male Bittern *Botaurus stellaris* and having the functions of a SONG. It is reminiscent of the noise produced by blowing sharply across the mouth of an empty bottle.

Booted   See SCUTELLATE(D).

Boreal   Having a northerly DISTRIBUTION or, more specifically, occurring in the region covered by the BOREAL FOREST.

Boreal Forest   The great belt of CONIFEROUS trees which stretches right across the northern continents to the south of the zone of Arctic TUNDRA. It is often called the 'taiga'. Birds of the Boreal Forest which regularly winter in the British Isles include the Redwing *Turdus iliacus* and the Crossbill *Loxia curvirostra*.

Botulism   A bacterial disease causing acute food poisoning, occurring particularly in stagnant water and so especially affecting WILDFOWL, hence the name 'duck sickness'. Serious outbreaks can cause very high MORTALITY among birds.

Brackish   See SALINE.

Brailing   The practice of preventing a bird from flying by tying the wing so that it is impossible for the bird to open it fully.

Breast   The part of a bird's exterior between the THROAT and the BELLY. The upper part of the breast may be called the 'chest'.

Breast band   A more or less broad zone of colour across the BREAST. It is also known as a 'pectoral band' or a 'gorget'. The Lapwing *Vanellus vanellus* has a black breast band; the Ring Ousel *Turdus torquatus* has a white one.

Breastbone   See STERNUM.

Breck   See HEATH.

Breeding biology   The study of all aspects of the BREEDING CYCLE.

Breeding cycle   The complete sequence of reproductive activity from initial COURTSHIP and pair formation through nesting to the final independence of the young.

Breeding distribution or **breeding range**   See DISTRIBUTION.

Breeding season   The time of year when reproduction takes place. Its beginning is rather indeterminate, as activities which form part of the BREEDING CYCLE, such as COURTSHIP and the establishment of a TERRITORY, may precede actual nesting by many weeks. The season ends for most SPECIES with the break-up of territories and DISPERSAL of the ADULT birds and their young.

Breeding success   The ability of a pair or a POPULATION to rear young to the flying stage.

Breeding territory   See TERRITORY.

BRIDLED GUILLEMOT

Bridled Guillemot   A form of the Guillemot *Uria aalge* with a white EYE RING and a thin white line extending behind the eye. It is not regarded as a SUBSPECIES, but merely as an example of DIMORPHISM. Bridled Guillemots may also be called 'Ringed Guillemots'. Their proportion in British colonies increases northwards.

Brightness factor   See LIGHT-GATHERING POWER.

British Association of Nature Conservationists   An organisation founded in 1979 to bring together the full range of those interested in the CONSERVATION of plants, animals and the natural ENVIRONMENT. It publishes the quarterly journal 'Ecos'.

'British Birds'   A monthly magazine for birdwatchers, covering all aspects of ornithology, with some emphasis on identification and RARITY recording. It is partly SCIENTIFIC and partly informal, and is illustrated with photographs and drawings. 'BB' is closely connected with the 'official' side of British ornithology and publishes the annual reports of the RARE BREEDING BIRDS PANEL and its own RARITIES COMMITTEE. The journal was founded in 1907 by H. F. Witherby, publisher and principal author of *The Handbook of British Birds* (1941). Since 1980, 'BB' has been published by its four-man editorial board from Fountains, Park Lane, Blunham, Bedford.

British Falconers' Club   See FALCONRY.

British Library of Wildlife Sounds   A collection of animal (largely bird) sound recordings, founded in 1969 and kept at the headquarters of the British Institute of Recorded Sound in London. It has a worldwide coverage and includes the work of such leading exponents of the art as Ludwig Koch.

British List   The 'official' list of bird SPECIES which have been recorded wild in the British Isles, properly called the 'British and Irish List'. It is kept by the BRITISH ORNITHOLOGISTS' UNION and the IRISH WILDBIRD CONSERVANCY. See Appendix D.

British Naturalists' Association   An organisation founded in 1905 with interests in the study and CONSERVATION of wildlife and its ENVIRONMENT. It publishes the journal 'Country-side' three times a year.

British Ornithologists' Club   A small organisation founded in 1880 and drawing its members only from the ranks of the BRITISH ORNITHOLOGISTS' UNION. It holds six dinners a year and publishes a quarterly bulletin containing short SCIENTIFIC papers. Its headquarters are at the ZOOLOGICAL SOCIETY OF LONDON.

British Ornithologists' Union   The 'official' (and oldest) British ornithological organisation, founded in 1858. Its purpose is the advancement of the SCIENTIFIC study of birds anywhere in the world, and this academic and international outlook is reflected in its quarterly journal 'The Ibis'. The BOU is the keeper of the official BRITISH LIST. Its headquarters are at the ZOOLOGICAL SOCIETY OF LONDON.

British Trust for Conservation Volunteers   An organisation founded in 1970 to provide practical assistance for public and private bodies and for individual landowners involved in CONSERVATION work. It has a large 'conservation corps' of volunteers, and supplies training and equipment where necessary. The Trust publishes a quarterly newsletter and has eight regional offices, with its headquarters at Reading in Berkshire.

British Trust for Ornithology   An organisation founded in 1933 to cater mainly for the serious amateur ornithologist. It is well-known for its co-operative surveys, both those which are repeated each year, such as the COMMON BIRDS CENSUS and the NEST RECORD SCHEME, and those relating to a particular period, notably the collection of field data for *The Atlas of Breeding Birds in Britain and Ireland*, which was published in 1976. The BTO is responsible for the administration of the British RINGING SCHEME and its staff are involved in many fields of ornithological research. It produces the thrice-yearly journal 'Bird Study' which contains scientific papers, the annual publication 'Ringing and Migration' and the bulletin 'BTO News' six times a year. Its headquarters are at Tring in Hertfordshire.

Broad   A shallow lake formed in a depression caused by mediaeval peat digging. Broads are mainly found in north-east Norfolk, and despite disturbance by holidaymakers are of great importance for WETLAND birds, notably the Bittern *Botaurus stellaris* and the Bearded Tit *Panurus biarmicus*.

Broad-front migration   Long-distance movement in which the birds are spread over wide areas instead of being confined to relatively narrow 'corridors'. This pattern of MIGRATION is typical of birds which are not limited to specialised kinds of HABITAT, and so is found, for example, in common PASSERINE birds where they are not constrained by physical features such as mountain passes. These, together with river valleys and coastlines, encourage 'narrow-front migration'.

Broad-leaved   Having blade-like rather than needle-like leaves, the converse of CONIFEROUS. It is not synonymous with DECIDUOUS, as some broad-leaved trees are evergreen (and some conifers are deciduous). Broad-leaved woodland of the 'deciduous summer forest' type forms the NATURAL VEGETATION of most parts of the British Isles.

Broken-wing trick See DISTRACTION DISPLAY.

Brood The young hatched from a single CLUTCH of eggs.

Brooding The warming of the eggs or young by the parent bird sitting over them. It is necessary because of the small size of the young, which causes them to lose heat relatively quickly, and, in NIDICOLOUS nestlings, because of their lack of THERMOREGULATION.

Brood nest A resting place for young birds built by one or both of the parents. It may or may not be the nest in which the brood was hatched. Construction of brood nests is found, for example, in the Moorhen *Gallinula chloropus*.

Brood parasite A bird which does not build a nest of its own but instead lays its eggs in the nests of birds of other SPECIES. The only example breeding in the British Isles is the Cuckoo *Cuculus canorus*, its most frequent 'hosts' or 'dupes' being the Meadow Pipit *Anthus pratensis* and the Dunnock *Prunella modularis*.

Brood patch A bare area on a bird's underside which develops at the time of year when the eggs require INCUBATION. It is completely free of DOWN and other feathers and is well supplied with blood vessels. Birds may have from one to three brood patches according to their SPECIES, although some have none, such as the Gannet *Sula bassana*, which warms its single egg with its webbed feet.

Buccal Of the mouth.

Bulla A bulbous extension to the SYRINX.

Busking The aggressive DISPLAY of the male Mute Swan *Cygnus olor* in which he advances across the water towards an intruder with his neck drawn back and his wings arched, proceeding with a jerky movement because during this display, as opposed to normal practice, he paddles with both feet in unison.

Butcher bird See LARDER

Butterfly flight A slow, fluttering and often erratic type of DISPLAY FLIGHT found, for example, in the Ringed Plover *Charadrius hiaticula*.

Caecum See INTESTINE.

Cagebird An individual or a SPECIES kept in captivity. Some species which occur wild in the British Isles are popular as cagebirds, notably some of the finches (FAMILY Fringillidae), but CLOSE RINGING is accepted as proof that they were bred in captivity and that their keeper has not broken the PROTECTION LAWS. Problems can be caused when a bird seen in the wild could be a naturally occurring VAGRANT, but could also be an ESCAPE from captivity. The keeping of cagebirds is called AVICULTURE.

Cain and Abel situation   Attack by the larger of two nestlings on the smaller. The size discrepancy is the result of ASYNCHRONOUS HATCH- ING and the 'Cain and Abel' situation is best seen in the Golden Eagle *Aquila chrysaetos*, which normally produces two young of which the smaller is often killed by the larger. As the obvious explanations, such as lack of sufficient food or INNATE aggressiveness, do not appear to explain this BEHAVIOUR, there is much debate as to its cause.

Calamus   See RACHIS.

Call   Any vocal sound produced by a bird which cannot be regarded as SONG, for example a CONTACT CALL or an alarm note.

Cannon net   See ROCKET NET.

Canopy   The branching parts of trees, forming the TREE LAYER in woodland. Where the canopy is continuous, the trees being close together, it is said to be 'closed', while an 'open' canopy is found where the trees do not touch each other.

Cap   A patch of colour covering the CROWN. A cap may extend below the eye, in which case it may almost become a HOOD, and it may also extend on to the NAPE or the HIND NECK. Examples of caps can be found in most terns (FAMILY Sternidae), which have black ones, and in the red cap of the Green Woodpecker *Picus viridis*.

Carina   See STERNUM.

Carnivorous   Eating the flesh of VERTEBRATE animals. Although a RAPTOR or an owl (ORDER Strigiformes) forms the obvious example of a carnivore among birds, others also qualify for this description, for example the PISCIVOROUS types, the shrikes (FAMILY Laniidae) and the crows (family Corvidae).

Carpal joint   The 'wrist' of a bird, forming the bend in the wing, between the ARM and the HAND.

Carr   Woodland growing in waterlogged conditions and consisting of trees such as willows and alders, well seen in the BROAD country of Norfolk. Its bird community resembles that of other BROAD-LEAVED woodland.

Casting   See PELLET.

Casual (species)   See VAGRANT.

Catching box   See HELIGOLAND TRAP.

Category A, B, C and D   The divisions of the BRITISH LIST into which SPECIES are grouped according to their STATUS in the British Isles. The use of these categories is explained in Appendix D of this book.

Caudal Of the tail.

Census A survey of the POPULATION of a given geographical area. A census consists of a series of counts, often involving many participants organised on a co-operative basis. The best example is the COMMON BIRDS CENSUS of the BRITISH TRUST FOR ORNITHOLOGY.

Central focusing The system of altering the focus of a pair of binoculars by turning a centrally placed wheel or drum which focuses each EYEPIECE simultaneously. The alternative arrangement, '(independent) eyepiece focusing', involves turning each eyepiece separately and is seldom found in modern instruments.

CERE : PEREGRINE

Cere A structure made of skin situated at the base of the upper MANDIBLE and containing the nostrils. This feature is found, for example, in the RAPTOR groups.

Cervical Of the neck.

Chardonneret trap A device for catching small birds, set off by the bird entering the trap. It is now used to catch birds for RINGING, originally for caging. The name is derived from the French word for Goldfinch *Carduelis carduelis*.

Charm A flock of Goldfinches *Carduelis carduelis*.

Chat One of the smaller members of the thrush FAMILY (Turdidae). The name refers to the Whinchat *Saxicola rubetra* and the Stonechat *S. torquata*, but it may be more loosely applied to cover such birds as the Redstart *Phoenicurus phoenicurus* and the Wheatear *Oenanthe oenanthe*.

Check list A list of SPECIES with space provided so that they can be ticked off as they are seen. Check lists are published by the journal BRITISH BIRDS, by the BRITISH TRUST FOR ORNITHOLOGY and by the ROYAL SOCIETY FOR THE PROTECTION OF BIRDS.

Cheek   See MALAR REGION.

Chin   The part of a bird's exterior immediately below the bill and above the THROAT.

Chipping   The breaking of the eggshell prior to hatching. The first sign is the appearance of cracks radiating from the point of the first breakthrough ('starring'). The chick then enlarges the cracks with its EGG TOOTH. An egg can be chipping for a period of a few hours or more than a day before the young bird is free of the shell.

Chitinous   Made of the hard horny substance ('chitin') of which the external skeletons of insects are composed. A bird PELLET may contain chitinous fragments from the insects which have been eaten.

Chord   The distance between the CARPAL JOINT and the tip of the longest PRIMARY (FEATHER), measured with the wing folded and pressed flat.

Chromatic aberration   The occurrence of a colour fringe or 'rainbow effect' in binoculars and telescopes around the edges of a dark object viewed against a very light background through an instrument of poor quality.

Churring   Producing a continuous deep TRILL. The best example to be heard in the British Isles is the SONG of the Nightjar *Caprimulgus europaeus*, which can be sustained for up to five minutes without a break, but many other SPECIES have churring CALL notes, for example the Mistle Thrush *Turdus viscivorus*.

Circadian rhythm   A cycle of activity which lasts (literally) 'about a day'. As most birds are affected by the alternation of day and night, their lives have circadian rhythms, but for coastal birds a tidally induced rhythm may be superimposed. There is a close connection between circadian rhythms and PHOTOPERIODISM.

Clap net   A device for trapping birds which consists of a net (of a size up to, perhaps, 7 × 3 metres) kept in a furled position for release by a pull-cord. When a group of birds moves into the catching area, the net is released and is thus thrown over the birds. In catching birds for RINGING, clap nets can be useful where the birds feed on the ground out in the open, as with WADER flocks on the shore. A much larger-scale development of the clap net is the ROCKET NET.

Class   The division in TAXONOMY which stands between the PHYLUM and the ORDER. All birds are placed in the class Aves.

Classification   See TAXONOMY.

Clavicle   See PECTORAL GIRDLE.

Climax vegetation   See SERE.

Cline   See SUBSPECIES.

Clipping   Cutting the PRIMARY feathers of one wing so that a bird is unable to fly. At the next MOULT it will grow new primaries and so will regain the power of flight. A permanent method of preventing a bird from flying is PINIONING.

Cloaca   The lower end of the ALIMENTARY SYSTEM, through which the FAECES is passed and the eggs are laid. The exterior opening is the 'anus' or 'vent'.

Closed canopy   See CANOPY.

Close ringing   Placing a ring on a bird's leg at the stage when its foot is still small enough for the ring to be slipped over it, so that a 'closed' ring can be used instead of one in the form of a strip which has to be closed with a pair of RINGING PLIERS. Close RINGING is the method used in AVICULTURE, and a bird ringed in this way can be regarded as having a captive origin.

Close season   See OPEN SEASON.

Clumping   Huddling together in a ROOST in order to conserve body heat. It is characteristic of very small SPECIES in winter or when young, examples being the Wren *Troglodytes troglodytes* and the Long-tailed Tit *Aegithalos caudatus*. These tiny birds lose heat more quickly than larger ones.

Clutch   A set of eggs laid by a single female in a single nesting attempt. In ornithological 'shorthand' a clutch of three eggs may be written 'c/3'. Clutch size can vary considerably in a SPECIES which is not a DETERMINATE LAYER, and in some cases DUMP NESTING can produce apparently very large clutches.

Cob   The male swan (GENUS *Cygnus*), the female being the 'pen'.

Cock's nest   A nest built by a male bird as part of the COURTSHIP ritual. Several such nests may be built by one male, one of which will be selected by the female. This BEHAVIOUR is well seen in the Wren *Troglodytes troglodytes*.

Coition   See COPULATION.

Cold searching   The practice of attempting to find nests simply by looking in suitable places. It is most successful where NEST SITE potential is limited. 'Hot searching' consists of trying to FLUSH a bird during INCUBATION, usually by lightly tapping the vegetation with a stick. This method would be useful where birds are nesting in thick cover, but does not comply with the BIRDWATCHER'S CODE OF CONDUCT.

Collecting   Killing a bird with the intention of preserving its SKIN as a specimen. Although collecting had its place in the past, today it is made unnecessary by the existence of adequate museum collections, so that reference material no longer need be acquired, and by the development of improved optical aids and field techniques, so that the bird in the hand is seldom required for identification. Indeed, under the bird PROTECTION LAWS, killing of most SPECIES is now illegal in the British Isles.

Colonisation   Extension of the breeding DISTRIBUTION of a SPECIES by natural means (rather than by INTRODUCTION). A rapid colonisation of an area is called an INVASION. Among recent colonists of Britain are the Savi's Warbler *Locustella luscinioides,* which was first proved to breed in 1960, and the Cetti's Warbler *Cettia cetti,* for which breeding was first proved in 1972.

Colony   An assembly of birds for breeding. Truly colonial SPECIES like the Gannet *Sula bassana* and the Rook *Corvus frugilegus* breed in dense agglomerations, while others can be described as 'semi-colonial' and nest in 'loose colonies', examples being the Lapwing *Vanellus vanellus* and the Goldfinch *Carduelis carduelis.*

Colour dyeing   A method of MARKING birds in which parts of their PLUMAGE are dyed a conspicuous colour, so that they can be recognised as belonging to a particular POPULATION and their movements can be followed. The dyed feathers will be lost at the next MOULT, so this is only a temporary method of marking. Colour dyeing is only suitable for relatively large birds, and has been much used on Bewick's Swans *Cygnus columbianus.*

Colour phase   See DIMORPHISM and POLYMORPHISM.

Colour ringing   See RINGING.

Comb   See WATTLE.

Comfort movement   An action which contributes to a bird's physical and mental well-being, for example PREENING, scratching and bathing.

Commensal   Eating the same food as another animal. Birds which raid crop fields, such as Woodpigeons *Columba palumbus,* are partly commensal with man. An animal whose whole life depends on another is a PARASITE, while one which obtains food simply as a result of the activities of another is practising AUTOLYCISM.

Commensural point   See GAPE.

Commic Tern   A Common Tern *Sterna hirundo* or an Arctic Tern *S. paradisaea,* the name being used on those occasions when the observer is uncertain which of these two closely similar SPECIES he has seen.

Common Birds Census   A survey organised annually by the BRITISH TRUST FOR ORNITHOLOGY in which observers plot the positions at which SONG of common birds is heard on large scale maps so that the TERRITORY of each pair can be roughly worked out, thus giving an indication of numbers and POPULATION density for the CENSUS areas. Population trends can thus be monitored when results are compared from year to year. Farmland and woodland are the main HABITAT types covered by the survey.

Community   A group of plants and animals with some feature in common, usually their HABITAT, as in 'the oakwood community' or 'the cliff-breeding community'.

Confidence limits   See STANDARD ERROR.

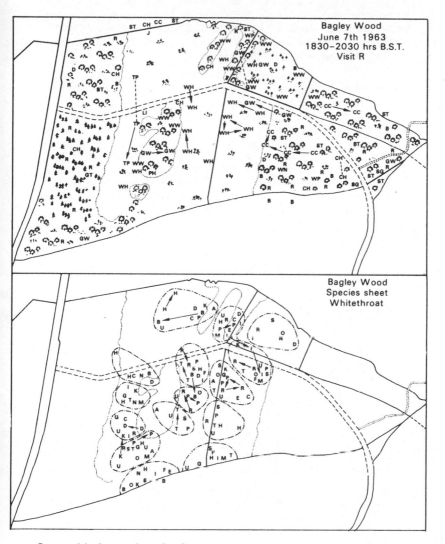

Bagley Wood
June 7th 1963
1830–2030 hrs B.S.T.
Visit R

Bagley Wood
Species sheet
Whitethroat

Census visit sheet and species sheet – see COMMON BIRDS CENSUS, opposite

Confirmed breeding See POSSIBLE BREEDING.

Congeneric Belonging to the same GENUS. The SPECIES which are placed in a particular genus are known as 'congeners'.

Coniferous Cone-bearing, with needle-like rather than blade-like leaves. It is not the converse of DECIDUOUS, because some conifers, for example the larch, are deciduous, but it is the converse of BROAD-LEAVED. Most British coniferous woods are plantations of EXOTIC trees. A few birds are particularly associated with conifers, examples being the Coal Tit *Parus ater* and the crossbills (GENUS *Loxia*).

Conservation The maintenance of a balance between the natural resources of the earth and man's use of them. Bird conservation is inseparable from nature conservation in general, in which the principles of ECOLOGY are applied in attempting to ensure that wild plants and animals are not adversely affected by human activities. The most fundamental need is the conservation of the various HABITAT types, and in practice nature conservation consists largely of efforts to protect vulnerable habitats, particularly by the use of the NATURE RESERVE. The chief British bird conservation agency is the ROYAL SOCIETY FOR THE PROTECTION OF BIRDS, whose functions in the Republic of Ireland are the responsibility of the IRISH WILDBIRD CONSERVANCY.

Conspecific Belonging to the same SPECIES.

Contact call A noise made by a bird as a means of keeping in touch with others of its SPECIES. The high-pitched calls of tits (FAMILY Paridae) as they move through a wood, and the twittering flight calls of finches (family Fringillidae) are examples.

Contour feather A body feather, as opposed to a wing or tail feather.

Control In a SCIENTIFIC experiment an individual or POPULATION which is monitored but not experimented upon. Assuming the control to be affected only by normal factors of its ENVIRONMENT, the effects of those factors which are allowed to act on the experimental population can thus be seen. The term has a different meaning in bird RINGING.

Convergence or **convergent evolution** The situation where two unrelated SPECIES or groups have developed in the course of EVOLUTION a similar ADAPTATION to their ENVIRONMENT, because they live in the same HABITAT and have evolved a similar life style. Swifts (FAMILY Apodidae) and swallows (family Hirundinidae) are good examples, while webbed feet have been developed by several groups of AQUATIC birds.

Copulation The sexual union of male and female which leads to the fertilisation of the egg ('ovum') by the male's sperms ('spermatozoa'). It is also called 'coition'. In order to copulate MOUNTING of the female bird by the male is necessary.

Coracoid See PECTORAL GIRDLE.

Corridor   See BROAD-FRONT MIGRATION.

Corvid   A member of the crow FAMILY (Corvidae).

Cosmopolitan   Found in every ZOOGEOGRAPHICAL REGION of the world. Examples of cosmopolitan SPECIES are the Osprey *Pandion haliaetus* and the Barn Owl *Tyto alba*.

Coues' Redpoll   See HORNEMANN'S REDPOLL.

Council for Environmental Conservation   An organisation founded in 1969 to bring together nature CONSERVATION societies and to promote their common interests. In 1979 it took over the functions of the Council for Nature, which had been founded in 1958 to act as an 'umbrella' body for British NATURAL HISTORY societies. CoEnCo has continued to publish the Council for Nature's monthly bulletin, 'Habitat'.

Council for Nature   See COUNCIL FOR ENVIRONMENTAL CONSERVATION.

Countershading   The presence of colours on the upperparts which are darker than those on the underparts. This is the usual situation in birds, being an ADAPTATION against predators.

County Bird Recorder   See BIRD RECORDER.

County Bird Report   See BIRD REPORT.

County (Naturalists') Trust   See NATURALISTS' TRUST.

Court   See LEK.

Courtship   Establishment of the PAIR-BOND, accomplished by various types of DISPLAY which have the purposes of breaking down aggression between male and female and stimulating sexual interest.

Courtship feeding   The presentation of food by the male to the female. It may only have ritual significance in COURTSHIP, simply being a DISPLAY, but where it is done during INCUBATION it may be an important source of nourishment for the female. In the latter case 'courtship feeding' is a misleading term.

Coverts   Small feathers concealing the bases of larger ones, for example TAIL COVERTS and WING COVERTS, or, in the case of the EAR COVERTS, concealing the ear openings.

Covey   A group (usually a family group) of partridges (GENUS *Alectoris* or *Perdix*).

Cranial   Of the skull ('cranium').

Crazy flying   Erratic zig-zagging in low flight over ground or water, as found in the Lapwing *Vanellus vanellus*. It is distinct from the tumbling DISPLAY FLIGHT of the SPECIES, and has no obvious purpose.

Crêche behaviour   The situation where broods of ducklings are combined into large groups tended by females which may or may not include mothers of the young in the 'crêches'. This BEHAVIOUR is found in the Eider *Somateria mollissima*.

Crepuscular　Connected with dusk. The Woodcock *Scolopax rusticola* and the Nightjar *Caprimulgus europaeus* are described as being crepuscular rather than NOCTURNAL in their habits.

Crest　A tuft of feathers on the upper part of the head, also called a 'horn'. Many crests can be raised or lowered according to the psychological state of the birds. They vary from the unspectacular example of the Skylark *Alauda arvensis* to the long wispy one found in the Lapwing *Vanellus vanellus*.

Cripple　See WINGED.

Crop - An extension in the side of a bird's OESOPHAGUS, used mainly for food storage and having little digestive function. It is also called the 'ingluvies'. Crops are best developed in GALLINACEOUS birds, and are absent in some INSECTIVOROUS types.

Cross-fostering　Replacement of the eggs of one SPECIES by those of another (usually closely related), so that the young are reared by the 'wrong' parents. Experiments of this kind throw light on the development of inherited and learned BEHAVIOUR patterns and the relationships between species. Cross-fostering can also be used in attempts to re-establish a species in an area in which it has become EXTINCT.

Cryptic　Camouflaging. Cryptic colouration and patterning of ADULT birds, eggs and young is well seen in many ground-nesting SPECIES, for example the Ringed Plover *Charadrius hiaticula* and the Woodcock *Scolopax rusticola*. The term opposite in meaning to 'cryptic' is 'phaneric', which essentially means 'advertising'. In most of the ducks (FAMILY Anatidae), for example, the PLUMAGE of the males is phaneric for use in DISPLAY, whereas that of the females is cryptic to conceal them during INCUBATION.

Culmen　The ridge along the top of the upper MANDIBLE. Its length is often quoted as one of the body dimensions of birds.

Cursorial　Having the habit of running, well seen in GALLINACEOUS birds.

Dabbling duck　A duck (FAMILY Anatidae) which does not normally dive for food, but obtains it by picking it from the water surface ('dabbling'), by SURFACE-DIPPING or by UPENDING. Dabbling ducks consist essentially of the members of the TRIBE Anatini, for example the Teal *Anas crecca* and the Mallard *A. platyrhynchos*.

Dabchick An alternative name for the Little Grebe *Tachybaptus ruficollis*.

Dark-bellied Brent Goose The SUBSPECIES of the Brent Goose *Branta bernicla* which breeds mainly in Arctic Asia and has the SCIENTIFIC NAME *B.b. bernicla*, as opposed to the Pale-bellied Brent Goose *B.b. hrota*, which is the subspecies breeding in Arctic Canada, Greenland and Spitsbergen. Both races occur in the British Isles in winter, *bernicla* being found mainly in eastern Britain and *hrota* in Ireland and Western Scotland.

Dawn chorus The peak of bird SONG around sunrise. It is most obvious in spring and early summer, and is best heard in woodland. There is a less spectacular 'evening chorus'.

Deciduous Dropping the leaves for the winter. It is not the converse of CONIFEROUS, as some conifers, for example the larch, are deciduous. Nor is it synonymous with BROAD-LEAVED, as some broad-leaved trees, for example the holly, are evergreen. 'Deciduous summer forest' forms the NATURAL VEGETATION of most parts of the British Isles.

Decoy A model of a bird used by hunters to attract their quarry within gunshot range. Not to be confused with a DUCK DECOY, which is a trapping station.

Density-dependent Varying according to POPULATION density. The effects of disease or PREDATOR pressure on a population may act in a density-dependent way.

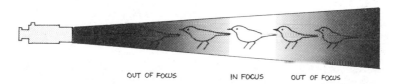

OUT OF FOCUS   IN FOCUS   OUT OF FOCUS

Depth of field or **depth of focus** The distance within which the image seen through a pair of binoculars or a telescope remains reasonably sharp and in focus. Generally, the higher the magnification, the further will be the nearest distance from the observer at which focusing becomes possible, so more powerful instruments usually have a reduced depth of field and a poorer close-focus performance and are less useful for watching nearby birds.

Descendant moult The usual sequence of MOULT in which the PRIMARY feathers are replaced from the CARPAL JOINT outwards. The other types of moult, 'ascendant' (from the outermost primary inwards), 'simultaneous' and 'irregular', are rarely found.

Determinate layer A SPECIES in which the female usually produces a fixed number of eggs in the CLUTCH. Various SEABIRD and WADER species are examples. Most birds, however, are 'indeterminate layers' to an extent which varies from one species to another.

Dialyt (binoculars)   See ROOF-PRISM BINOCULARS.

Diastataxic   Having no SECONDARY feather corresponding to the fifth feather of the greater WING COVERTS. If a secondary is present, the arrangement is called 'eutaxic'. Diastataxy occurs in grebes (FAMILY Podicipedidae), geese of the GENUS *Anser*, owls (ORDER Strigiformes) and pigeons (family Columbidae).

Digit   See PHALANGES.

Dimorphism   The existence of two distinctive forms (usually differing in terms of PLUMAGE colour) within a SPECIES, but not regarded as constituting separate SUBSPECIES. Sexual dimorphism is common, while some species have two 'colour phases' or 'morphs', for example the Fulmar *Fulmarus glacialis* and the Arctic Skua *Stercorarius parasiticus*, each of which has dark and light forms. Where more than two phases exist the situation is described as POLYMORPHISM.

Dipping out   Failing to see a rare bird which other birdwatchers have succeeded in seeing. This TWITCHING term emphasises the competitive element in RARITY hunting.

Direct head-scratching   See INDIRECT HEAD-SCRATCHING.

Dispersal   An outward movement from the breeding place at the end of the BREEDING SEASON, when TERRITORY is abandoned and birds disperse, either in a definite direction or apparently at random. This movement takes place before true MIGRATION begins.

Dispersion   The DISTRIBUTION of individuals, pairs or groups through an area.

Displacement activity   BEHAVIOUR which is inappropriate to a particular situation, indicating uncertainty or anxiety. Pecking at the ground and FALSE PREENING are examples. Head scratching in humans is a comparable activity.

Display   Ritualised BEHAVIOUR. Displays often emphasise bright patches of colour or other PLUMAGE features and frequently have a vocal component. They indicate excitement, aggression, fear and similar emotions and they evolved by means of the process of RITUALISATION.

Display flight   An aerial part of COURTSHIP, involving one or both of a pair, in which a special mode of flying and distinctive CALL notes may be used. A DISPLAY flight with a strong vocal component is a SONG FLIGHT. The BUTTERFLY FLIGHT of the Ringed Plover *Charadrius hiaticula* and the bat-like performance of the Greenfinch *Carduelis chloris* are examples of display flights.

Distal Situated furthest from the base, as in 'the distal part of a feather'. The converse is 'proximal'.

Distraction display Behaviour in which a bird disturbed from its eggs or young attempts to lure the intruder away from them by calling loudly and acting conspicuously, or even pretending to be injured (the 'broken-wing trick' or 'injury-feigning'). The distraction DISPLAY is found in some ground-nesting birds, notably certain types of WADER.

Distribution The pattern of occurrence of a SPECIES as seen when plotted on a map, also known as its 'range'. Each species has a 'breeding distribution', which only coincides with its distribution in winter if the species is truly SEDENTARY, as are few birds outside the tropics. A species which is wholly a SUMMER VISITOR to the British Isles is likely to have completely separate breeding and wintering distributions, for example the Swallow *Hirundo rustica*, occurring in the intervening regions only on PASSAGE.

Diurnal Occurring during the day, a term usually employed as the opposite of NOCTURNAL.

Diving duck A duck (FAMILY Anatidae) which habitually dives for food, as opposed to a DABBLING DUCK. The main groups of diving ducks found in the British Isles are the pochards (TRIBE Aythyini), the eiders (tribe Somateriini) and the scoters, goldeneyes and SAWBILL ducks (tribe Mergini).

Domestic(ated) Not found in the wild, having been developed by man. Some domestic forms have been bred from SPECIES which occur wild in the British Isles, and in cases where domestic and wild stock have interbred problems of definition arise. This situation particularly applies to the Mallard *Anas platyrhynchos*.

Domestic Pigeon See FERAL PIGEON.

DISPLAY : RINGED PLOVER

Dominance   The social hierarchy within and between SPECIES, also called 'peck order'. Within a species, males may be dominant over females, except perhaps at the nest, but females may dominate IMMATURE birds. Examples of dominance between species are Great Tit *Parus major* over Blue Tit *P. caeruleus* and Carrion Crow *Corvus corone* over Jackdaw *C. monedula*, in these cases dominance being apparently a matter of size.

Dominant species   See DOMINANCE.

Dorsal   Connected with the upper surface of the body. The opposite term, referring to the underparts, is 'ventral'.

Double-brooded   See SINGLE-BROODED.

Down   A type of feather where the shaft (RACHIS) is more or less absent and each BARB is long and fluffy. In ADULT birds down forms a kind of underwear beneath the main feathers, while chicks develop a covering of down ('natal down' or 'neossoptile' feathers) varying in thickness according to SPECIES. Down feathers may also be called 'plumules'. Their main function is insulation.

Downy   See NIDIFUGOUS.

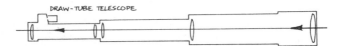

DRAW-TUBE TELESCOPE

Drawtube   The movable part of a non-PRISMATIC telescope, the tube being slid back and forth in order to focus the instrument.

Dread   See PANIC.

Drift migration   A type of movement in which a bird is forced away from its normal MIGRATION course by adverse winds. Easterly gales in autumn can bring continental drift migrants to the British Isles.

Drive   An attempt to persuade birds to enter a trap in order to catch them for RINGING. For example, small PASSERINE birds may be slowly driven into the wide mouth of a HELIGOLAND TRAP.

Drop net or **drop trap**   A device for trapping individual birds in which a net or cage falls over the bird when a pull-cord is operated. These nets or traps are sometimes used to catch birds for RINGING.

Drumming   Rapid tapping by the bill of a woodpecker (FAMILY Picidae) on a dead branch, or the sound of air passing through the spread tail feathers of a Snipe *Gallinago gallinago* as it dives during its DISPLAY FLIGHT (also known as 'bleating'). It is an example of INSTRUMENTAL SONG.

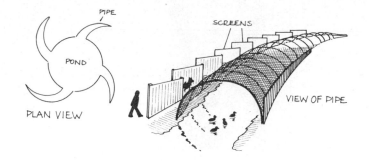

Duck decoy A device for catching ducks (FAMILY Anatidae), consisting of a pond, well screened by bushes and having several backwaters ('pipes') which gradually narrow away from the pond. A trained dog lures ducks from the pond along the pipe, then the decoyman appears behind them and drives them into a trap at the narrow end. A few duck decoys are still in operation to catch ducks for RINGING, for example the one in the WILDFOWL TRUST grounds at Slimbridge in Gloucestershire.

Duck sickness See BOTULISM.

Dude A casual birdwatcher, without a serious commitment. The term is used in TWITCHING.

Dump nesting The laying of eggs by one female in the nest of another, usually of the same SPECIES. It occurs particularly in the ducks (FAMILY Anatidae), and may account for some abnormally large CLUTCH sizes.

Dupe See BROOD PARASITE.

Dusky Redshank An alternative name for the Spotted Redshank *Tringa erythropus*.

Dust-bathing or **dusting** Forcing fine, dry material (such as dust or fine soil) into the PLUMAGE by squatting on the ground and making appropriate movements with the body, wings and legs. Like ANTING and SMOKE BATHING, dusting presumably discourages ECTOPARASITE infestation. It is characteristic of birds living in arid types of HABITAT, such as larks (FAMILY Alaudidae), but is also well known, for example, in the House Sparrow *Passer domesticus*.

Ear coverts The short feathers covering the ears, which have no external parts and are situated behind and slightly below the eyes.

EAR-TUFTS : LONG-EARED OWL

Ear tuft   A bunch of long feathers towards the top of the head found particularly in the Long-eared Owl *Asio otus*. They can be erected when the bird is excited or afraid but have nothing to do with the ears or with hearing. An ear tuft may also be called a 'horn'.

Ecdysis   See MOULT.

Eclipse   A type of PLUMAGE assumed by the drakes of most SPECIES of ducks (FAMILY Anatidae) during their period of MOULT in late summer and autumn. All WILDFOWL moult all their flight feathers at once, so that they become flightless for a time, and the eclipse plumage, which resembles the dull plumage of the females, renders the otherwise brightly coloured drakes inconspicuous during a stage when they are more vulnerable than usual to PREDATOR attack.

Ecological isolation   Separation of closely related SPECIES by their use of different HABITAT types or different parts of the same habitat. For example, the Blackbird *Turdus merula*, basically a woodland species, is largely isolated ecologically from its close relative the moorland-breeding Ring Ouzel *T. torquatus*.

Ecological niche   See NICHE.

Ecology   The study of the relationships between the living ORGANISM and all aspects of its ENVIRONMENT. If the ecological relationships involving a single SPECIES or group are being treated, the study is called 'autecology'. If a complete ECOSYSTEM is being studied, it is called 'synecology'.

Economic ornithology   The study of the effects of birds on man's activities, particularly where people's livelihoods are affected. Among the most important aspects are bird damage to farm crops and orchards, and the BIRD STRIKE danger at airfields.

Ecosystem   The complex web of relationships between a COMMUNITY and its ENVIRONMENT. It is the fundamental concept of ECOLOGY, and it can be studied at any scale. The whole world can be considered as one vast ecosystem as well as the sum total of a huge number of smaller ecosystems.

Ecotone   The transition zone between two types of HABITAT. For example, woodland edge is an ecotone standing between open country and forest habitats. Ecotones are usually richer in their variety of birds than the adjoining habitats as they contain a mixture of SPECIES from each habitat. This tendency is called 'edge effect'.

Ecotype   See HABITAT.

Ectoparasite   A PARASITE living on the outside of its host's body, as opposed to an ENDOPARASITE. Birds are subject to a great deal of infestation by ectoparasites on their skin and in their PLUMAGE and nests. The FEATHER LOUSE is a good example, but in addition there are other lice, fleas, mites and ticks.

Edge effect   See ECOTONE.

Edward Grey Institute (of Field Ornithology)   An academic research organisation founded in 1933, now part of the Zoology Department of the University of Oxford, and containing the ALEXANDER LIBRARY. It is named after the famous ornithologist Lord Grey of Falloden.

Eggbound   Unable to lay eggs even though they have been formed.

Egging   The removal of eggs from nests, now an illegal practice in the case of most SPECIES in the British Isles under the bird PROTECTION LAWS.

Egg pricking   Making a small hole in the shell of an egg, which eventually causes the death of the EMBRYO. Egg pricking is practised in situations where the POPULATION of a particular SPECIES on a NATURE RESERVE is growing at the expense of one or more other species which are in need of special protection. The owners of the pricked eggs continue with their INCUBATION, not realising that anything is amiss, and so they do not lay REPLACEMENT eggs. On coastal reserves the numbers of Black-headed Gulls *Larus ridibundus* may be controlled in this way.

Eggshell thinning   Reduction in the thickness of eggshells caused by TOXIC CHEMICAL residues in a bird's body and often resulting in egg breakage by the birds. Some types of RAPTOR have particularly suffered from this problem.

EGG TOOTH

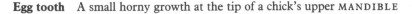

Egg tooth   A small horny growth at the tip of a chick's upper MANDIBLE used to break through the eggshell. This 'tooth' is lost within a few days of hatching.

Eiderdown   The DOWN feathers of the female Eider *Somateria mollissima* plucked from her underparts to line the nest and to cover the eggs. It is the best insulating material known and is collected commercially in some countries, notably Iceland.

Emarginate(d)   Having a 'cut away' effect, referring to the shape of the WEB of a feather.

Embryo   The initial stage of the development of the young within the egg. In a newly laid egg the embryo is a tiny speck surrounded by the food stores of the yolk and the 'white' (albumen).

Endangered species   A SPECIES which is likely to become EXTINCT if its POPULATION declines further. No species which breeds in the British Isles is in danger of worldwide extinction at present, but a few, for example the Wryneck *Jynx torquilla* and the Red-backed Shrike *Lanius collurio*, may well cease to be British breeders.

Endemic   Confined to a particular limited area. There is only one bird SPECIES which is endemic to the British Isles, namely the Scottish Crossbill *Loxia scotica*, although there are many endemic SUBSPECIES.

Endocrine gland   A HORMONE-producing ORGAN, also known as a 'ductless GLAND'. An example is the pituitary gland, which is situated underneath the brain. Collectively these glands form the 'endocrine system'.

Endogenous   Produced from within the body. The converse, meaning 'produced from outside the body', is 'exogenous'.

Endoparasite   A PARASITE living inside its host's body, as opposed to an ECTOPARASITE. Birds are subject to a great deal of infestation by endoparasites, the main types being cestodes (tapeworms), nematode and thorny-headed worms, trematodes (flukes) and the tiny protozoans.

Endysis   See MOULT.

Environment   The sum total of the external influences on a living ORGANISM. The term 'environmental' can scarcely be distinguished from 'ecological', and in relating birds to their environments the principles of ECOLOGY are of fundamental importance.

Epizootic   A large-scale outbreak of disease, being the equivalent of an 'epidemic' among humans. An example which regularly involves birds is BOTULISM.

Eruption   See IRRUPTION.

Erythrism   Excess of reddish pigment, giving an 'erythristic' individual an ABERRANT appearance. Erythrism is comparable with ALBINISM and MELANISM.

Escape An individual found in the wild but which originated in captivity, either having escaped or having been freed deliberately. The most frequent escapes are popular types of CAGEBIRD, like Budgerigars *Melopsittacus undulatus* and Canaries *Serinus canaria*, together with WILD-FOWL from outdoor collections. The FERAL Ruddy Ducks *Oxyura jamaicensis* and Ring-necked Parakeets *Psittacula krameri* found in Britain originated as escapes, and the former has been admitted to the BRITISH LIST. In the case of species which might occur naturally in a particular area but which are also kept in captivity, it is often difficult to decide whether a sighting refers to a genuinely wild bird or an escape, this problem being especially acute with geese (FAMILY Anatidae).

Estuary An inlet of the sea which is really the lower end of a river valley. At high tide the sea floods the estuary, but at low water areas of sand, MUD FLAT and SALTMARSH are revealed, providing a rich feeding ground for many types of WILDFOWL and WADER. The estuaries of the British Isles are of great importance to such birds, especially to those on MIGRATION to and from the European continent, but this HABITAT is greatly threatened by barrage schemes, land reclamation and industrialisation. Among the most important British estuaries are those of the Rivers Forth, Mersey and Medway.

Ethiopian (Region) See ZOOGEOGRAPHICAL REGION.

Ethology See BEHAVIOUR.

Euring The European Union for Bird Ringing, formed in the early 1960s to bring about international co-operation within Europe. The British RINGING SCHEME is a member. The RINGING RECOVERY codes used in computer processing of results in most European countries were ratified by Euring and a data bank has been set up to store the recovery details at Arnhem in the Netherlands. The EEC has provided a grant to enable the computerisation of historic records.

European Ornithological Atlas Committee See ATLASSING.

Eutaxic See DIASTATAXIC.

Eutrophic Rich in plant nutrients, usually referring to fresh water. Eutrophication can occur naturally or can be caused by residues of fertilisers draining into the water from farmland. The opposite term, referring to nutrient-poor waters, is 'oligotrophic'. Eutrophic conditions are much more favourable for birds than oligotrophic.

Evolution Development of the living ORGANISM through gradual changes in its characteristics by MUTATION over long periods of time. Thus one SPECIES may evolve into two or more different species, any of which, and/or the original species, may become EXTINCT. Evolution proceeds by means of NATURAL SELECTION and ADAPTIVE RADIATION.

Excretion The removal of waste substances from the blood by the kidneys, which form the 'excretory system', in the form of urine, which in birds is usually semi-liquid and creamy-white in colour. It is expelled with the FAECES through the CLOACA to form the droppings. In some birds excretion of excess salts is also possible through the SALT GLAND.

Exit pupil diameter See LIGHT-GATHERING POWER.

Exogenous See ENDOGENOUS.

Exotic Not INDIGENOUS to a particular area. Several exotic birds are found wild in the British Isles because of INTRODUCTION by man.

Exploding The rapid departure of nestlings of NIDICOLOUS birds from their nest if disturbed by a potential PREDATOR during the period just before they would normally leave. It is an ADAPTATION for survival, in that if the birds remained in the nest the predator would be likely to kill the entire BROOD, whereas exploding scatters the brood and so gives at least some of the young the chance to escape.

Extinct No longer breeding in a particular area. Although a number of bird SPECIES have become extinct in the British Isles during historical times, only one of these, the Great Auk *Pinguinus impennis*, has suffered worldwide extinction.

Extralimital Occurring only outside the boundaries of the area under consideration. For example, the Kittiwake *Rissa tridactyla* has a relative, the Red-legged Kittiwake *R. brevirostris*, which breeds only in the north Pacific and, so as far as Europe is concerned, would be described as extralimital.

Eyas(s) A young falcon (FAMILY Falconidae).

Eye cup A soft rubber ring on the EYEPIECE of a pair of binoculars which can be folded back so that a spectacle wearer can place his eye near enough to the lens to obtain the same FIELD OF VIEW as anyone else. Those binoculars which have this facility may be designated by the letter 'B', for example '10 × 40B'.

Eyepiece The part of a binocular or telescope to which the eye is placed, consisting of a series of lenses. It is by moving the position of the eyepiece that focusing is achieved, either by CENTRAL FOCUSING or by (independent) eyepiece focusing.

Eye ring A ring of colour around the eye, as seen, for example, in the male Blackbird *Turdus merula*. It is also called an 'orbital ring'.

Eye stripe A line 'through' a bird's eye, as seen, for example, in the Blue Tit *Parus caeruleus*.

Eyrie The nest or NEST SITE of a large RAPTOR such as the Golden Eagle *Aquila chrysaetos*.

FACIAL DISC : BARN OWL

Facial disc   A well defined, relatively flat, forward facing part of the head as seen in some owls (ORDER Strigiformes), notably the Barn Owl *Tyto alba*. It probably helps the bird in locating prey by sound, focusing the sounds made by the prey on the owl's ear openings.

Faecal analysis   See FAECES.

Faecal sac   A white jelly-like 'envelope' in which the FAECES of the nestlings of NIDICOLOUS birds is enclosed. It is easily removed from the nest by the parents, thus promoting efficient nest sanitation.

Faeces   The waste product from the ALIMENTARY SYSTEM, expelled through the CLOACA along with the urine, which is produced by EXCRETION from the kidneys. The faeces forms the dark part of a bird dropping. Faecal analysis can be useful in studying the food of birds but as in PELLET analysis it over-emphasises the intake of food items with hard indigestible parts.

Failed breeder   See NON-BREEDER.

Falcated   Sickle-shaped, as in some of the SCAPULAR feathers of the drake Pintail *Anas acuta*.

Falcon   Apart from its more general meaning, specifically the female of any SPECIES of the FAMILY Falconidae, the male being called the 'tiercel'.

Falconry   The practice of hunting with a trained RAPTOR, also known as 'hawking'. Some of its terms, such as EYAS(S) and TIERCEL, are used by birdwatchers. The British Falconers' Club, founded in 1927, seeks to maintain standards and to encourage the CONSERVATION of British raptors.

Fall   A sudden arrival of large numbers of birds at a certain point, usually coastal. Falls may occur when MIGRATION is interrupted by the rapid onset of adverse weather, such as gales or fog, and they involve mainly PASSERINE birds. At a BIRD OBSERVATORY a fall of migrants gives an opportunity for mass RINGING.

False preening   Apparent PREENING which, in fact, only involves the motions of true preening. It is a type of DISPLACEMENT ACTIVITY.

Family   The division in TAXONOMY which stands between the ORDER and (usually) the GENUS. The SCIENTIFIC NAME of a bird family always ends in '-idae', for example the family Fringillidae (finches).

Farming and Wildlife Advisory Group   An organisation founded in 1969 to bring together farmers and those involved in nature CONSERVATION with a view to mutual understanding. The group's headquarters are at those of the ROYAL SOCIETY FOR THE PROTECTION OF BIRDS, and there are many local committees.

Fault bar   A narrow band across the WEB of a feather, perhaps representing that part of the feather which grew during the later part of a night, hence the alternative terms 'starvation mark' and 'hunger trace'. Each feather so affected has a series of fault bars and they are probably present on most individuals.

Fauna   The animals (including birds) found in a particular area, or a description of them. The bird component of the fauna is called the 'avifauna'.

Faunal region   See ZOOGEOGRAPHICAL REGION.

Fauna Preservation Society   An organisation founded in 1909 and concerned with the worldwide conservation of animals. It publishes the thrice-yearly journal 'Oryx' and has its headquarters at the ZOOLOGICAL SOCIETY OF LONDON.

Faunistics   The classification of animals, a branch of TAXONOMY.

Feather louse   A member of the insect SUB-ORDER Mallophaga living as an ECTOPARASITE among a bird's feathers. These lice are very common among birds, feeding on the feathers themselves, and many are HOST-SPECIFIC. Birds are also likely to be infested with 'louse-flies', which have a characteristic flattened shape and feed by sucking blood. They are members of the FAMILY Hippoboscidae, hence the use of the term 'hippoboscids' to describe them.

Feather mite   A member of the arachnid ORDER Acari (which also contains the ticks) living as an ECTOPARASITE among a bird's feathers. These mites are very common among birds, and they feed on the feathers themselves and flakes of skin, rather than by sucking blood.

Feather tract   A part of a bird's skin from which feathers grow, the feathers being confined to these tracts (also called 'pterylae') and not growing all over the body, even though they normally provide a complete cover. There are typically eight feather tracts and a similar number of areas of bare skin.

Feeding niche   See NICHE.

Feeding station   Any point at which wild birds are deliberately and regularly fed by humans.

Feeding territory   See TERRITORY.

Femur   The thighbone, not held free of the body in birds.

Fen   See MARSH.

Feral   Living in a wild, self-maintaining state after having escaped, or been released, from captivity but still somewhat dependent on man. Apart from the FERAL PIGEON, examples of birds living ferally in the British Isles are the Canada Goose *Branta canadensis* and the Ring-necked Parakeet *Psittacula krameri*.

Feral Pigeon   A bird descended from DOMESTIC pigeon stock but living in a FERAL state. These birds are common both in towns and in the countryside and may be called 'domestic', 'homing', 'lodge', 'London' or 'town' pigeons as well as 'feral' pigeons. Despite a variety of colours all are ultimately descended from the wild Rock Dove *Columba livia* and interbreeding between wild and feral birds has blurred the distinction between them.

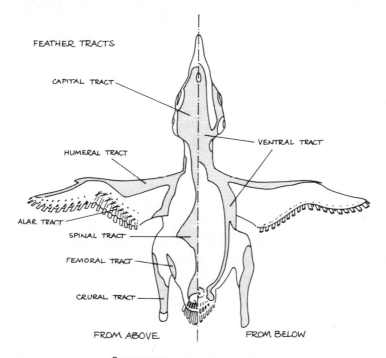

FEATHER TRACTS

CAPITAL TRACT

VENTRAL TRACT

HUMERAL TRACT

ALAR TRACT

SPINAL TRACT

FEMORAL TRACT

CRURAL TRACT

FROM ABOVE   FROM BELOW

See FEATHER TRACT, opposite

Fibula   One of the two bones of the shin or calf, the other being the 'tibiotarsus' in birds. This part of the bird's leg is partly hidden by feathers, being above the backward-facing TARSAL JOINT.

Field centre   An establishment which offers courses in those subjects which can be studied in the field, notably various branches of BIOLOGY and NATURAL HISTORY. A field centre may be operated on a charitable basis, as a public service or as a commercial enterprise. An organisation well known for its field centres is the FIELD STUDIES COUNCIL.

Field character   A feature which is sufficiently distinctive to enable a particular SPECIES to be identified by means of it in the field. It may be a PLUMAGE characteristic (also called a 'field mark') (such as the red BREAST of the Robin *Erithacus rubecula*), a sound (such as the SONG of the Cuckoo *Cuculus canorus*), or a habit (such as the tail-cocking of the Wren *Troglodytes troglodytes*).

Field guide   A pocket-sized book intended to be taken into the field by the birdwatcher to enable identification of birds to be made on the spot. Field guides are well illustrated in colour with texts virtually confined to identification points. The first example was published in the USA in 1934, written and illustrated by Roger Tory Peterson, but the first British field guide, by R. S. R. Fitter and R. A. Richardson, did not appear until 1952. There are now three standard field guides covering the whole of Europe, namely, those by Roger Peterson, Guy Mountfort and P. A. D. Hollom (first published 1954); by Bertel Bruun and Arthur Singer (first published 1970); and by Herman Heinzel, Richard Fitter and John Parslow (first published 1972), the latter's coverage extending to North Africa and the Middle East.

Field layer   The zone of vegetation up to two metres in height which lies above the GROUND LAYER and below the SHRUB LAYER, if there is one. It consists essentially of non-woody plants, and is also called the 'herb layer'.

Field mark   See FIELD CHARACTER.

Field of view   The width of the picture seen through a pair of binoculars or a telescope, expressed as a segment in degrees or, more usually, as so many metres at a distance of 1,000 metres. The higher the magnification the smaller the field of view will be if the size and weight of the instrument are to be kept within reasonable limits.

Field Studies Council   An organisation founded in 1943 to promote all kinds of outdoor studies. It organises the type of courses which are based on a FIELD CENTRE. The Council's headquarters are at Montford Bridge in Shropshire, and it has nine field centres in various parts of England and Wales. Its counterpart in Scotland is the Scottish Field Studies Association, which was founded in 1945 and is based near Blairgowrie in Perthshire.

Filoplume   A hairlike feather consisting of a shaft (RACHIS) only, with no WEB. Such feathers are scattered thinly over a bird's body.

Fingers   Wing-tip feathers which become widely separated during flight, as seen in members of the crow FAMILY (Corvidae).

Fixed action pattern   An inborn sequence of BEHAVIOUR in which variations do not normally occur. An example is the opening of the GAPE by young nestlings when their nest is touched, irrespective of what has touched it.

Flank   The side of a bird's BELLY, appearing immediately below the forepart of the closed wing. The flanks may have a distinctive pattern or colour, as in the Water Rail *Rallus aquaticus* and Redwing *Turdus iliacus* respectively.

Flash   A small lake or marsh caused by flooding, with particular reference to those resulting from mining subsidence. The term is used on the Cheshire saltfield and on the Lancashire and Derbyshire coalfields, but in Yorkshire it is replaced by the word 'ing'. Flashes may have considerable ornithological interest, and Fairburn Ings in West Yorkshire is an important NATURE RESERVE.

Fledge   See FLEDGLING.

Fledgling   A young bird which has just left the nest ('fledged'). The term is used of NIDICOLOUS young, which leave their nests only when they are fully feathered and ready to fly.

Flight   A regular aerial movement between two places or over a certain area. Flightlines used by gulls (FAMILY Laridae) or starlings *Sturnus vulgaris* between a ROOST and feeding grounds may be particularly well defined.

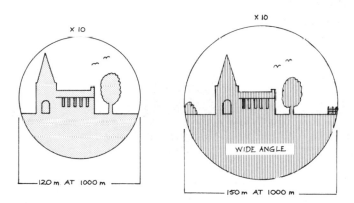

Fields of view with normal and wide angle binoculars or telescopes of the same magnification – see FIELD OF VIEW, opposite

Flight feather See PRIMARY (FEATHER), SECONDARY (FEATHER), and TERTIARY (FEATHER).

Flightline See FLIGHT.

Flight muscle See PECTORAL MUSCLES.

Flow See MARSH.

Flush Cause a bird to take flight.

Flyway A major route for birds on MIGRATION. An important flyway runs down the west coast of Europe and includes the British Isles. The flyway concept is further developed in North America than in Europe.

Food cache A concealed store of food. A few SPECIES, such as the Coal Tit *Parus ater* and the Jay *Garrulus glandarius*, are known to make such caches, Jays often burying considerable quantities of acorns. The birds are able to find at least some of this stored food, which presumably has survival value for them during periods of food shortage in winter.

Food chain A series of links between plants and animals expressed as feeding relationships in linear form. For example, if a slug feeds on vegetation and is then eaten by a thrush (GENUS *Turdus*), which is in turn taken by a Sparrowhawk *Accipiter nisus*, the resulting food chain would be as follows: vegetation – slug – thrush – hawk. Each link in the chain is called a 'trophic level' and in this particular example the hawk is the 'top PREDATOR'. In reality the concept of a 'food web' is more valid than that of a food chain, as few animals have a single food source.

Food pass Aerial food presentation by the male of a RAPTOR pair to the female, usually taking place during the periods of COURTSHIP, IN-CUBATION and BROODING of the young.

Food piracy See KLEPTOPARASITISM.

Food web See FOOD CHAIN.

Foot-paddling See PADDLING.

FRONTAL SHIELD : WHITE FRONTED GOOSE

Forehead The front part of the CROWN, extending down to the base of the bill. It may be distinctively coloured, as in the white (unfeathered) 'frontal shield' of the White-fronted Goose *Anser albifrons* and in the red (feathered) forehead of the Redpoll *Carduelis flammea.*

Form   A hollow in low vegetation made by the body of a bird (such as a Grey Partridge *Perdix perdix*) using the spot as a ROOST.

Fossorial   Having the habit of digging. The term is applied to those birds which excavate nest holes in the ground, such as the Kingfisher *Alcedo atthis* and the Sand Martin *Riparia riparia.*

French Partridge   An alternative name for the Red-legged Partridge *Alectoris rufa.*

Frontal shield   See FOREHEAD.

Frugivorous   Fruit-eating. The thrushes (FAMILY Turdidae) are examples of frugivores.

Full-winged   Having the power of flight, rather than deprived of it by MOULT of the wing feathers or by BRAILING, CLIPPING or PINION-ING.

Fulmar oil   An evil-smelling oily substance ejected by the Fulmar *Fulmarus glacialis* as a defence against a PREDATOR. It originates in the stomach and may have food mixed with it.

Furcula   See PELVIC GIRDLE.

Gaggle   A group of geese (FAMILY Anatidae) on the ground, a flying flock being called a SKEIN.

Gallinaceous   Belonging to the ORDER Galliformes, which in the British Isles contains the FAMILY Tetraonidae (grouse) and the family Phasianidae (partridges and pheasants). A gallinaceous bird may also be called a GAME BIRD.

Game bird   A bird which may legally be shot during its particular OPEN SEASON. Although the term is often used simply to refer to GALLINACEOUS birds, in fact game birds include many SPECIES of WILDFOWL, the Moorhen *Gallinula chloropus*, the Coot *Fulica atra* and a few species of WADER.

Gape   The mouth, namely the space between the upper MANDIBLE and the lower. The angle of the gape is called the 'commensural point'. An AERIAL FEEDER has a particularly wide gape, as does a NIDICOLOUS nestling, in the latter case outlined by colourful 'gape flanges', presumably to guide the parent when thrusting in food.

Gape flange   See GAPE.

Gapes   A disease caused by an infestation of 'gapeworms' in the

TRACHEA, the ENDOPARASITE concerned being a red nematode. It particularly affects the Starling *Sturnus vulgaris* and the Rook *Corvus frugilegus*.

Gardening The practice of tying back the vegetation round a nest and otherwise re-arranging it so that the birds can be more easily photographed. It is important that after the photography has been completed the vegetation is replaced in its original position, in case the gardening has facilitated the attack of a PREDATOR.

Gause's Principle The theory that two SPECIES cannot share exactly the same HABITAT, for otherwise in the course of time one would have eliminated the other through NATURAL SELECTION.

Gene See GENETIC.

Genera See GENUS.

Generic name See BINOMIAL NOMENCLATURE and GENUS.

Genetic Concerned with heredity (the acquisition of characteristics by the young from their parents), the study of which is called 'genetics'. A parent transmits to its offspring the blueprints of inherited characters in units called 'genes', a particular genetic arrangement being called a 'genotype'.

Genotype See GENETIC.

Gens (plural gentes) A group within a SPECIES sharing a common characteristic. For example, in the Cuckoo *Cuculus canorus* a number of gentes exist, each a PARASITE on a particular host species.

Genus (plural genera) The division in TAXONOMY which stands between the FAMILY and the SPECIES. The name of the genus (the 'generic name') appears as the first part of the SCIENTIFIC NAME of each of its member species, under the rules of BINOMIAL NOMENCLATURE.

Gizzard The stomach of a bird, part of the ALIMENTARY SYSTEM. It has thick muscular walls and may contain grit which has been deliberately swallowed to grind up food particles, in the absence of the ability to chew.

Gland An ORGAN which produces a SECRETION, for example an ENDOCRINE GLAND.

Glaucous Greyish-blue.

Gliding Flying with the wings stiffly outstretched instead of being flapped. Birds glide between wing beats or when descending, or when rising against the wind. Gliding involves travelling in a more or less straight line, circling in rising air currents ('thermals') being called 'soaring'. Whereas a wide variety of birds glide, those which soar have long relatively narrow wings, for example some types of RAPTOR and the gulls (FAMILY Laridae). Soaring is useful for saving energy while scanning the ground for prey or other food and while on MIGRATION.

Gloger's Rule The contention that for a given SPECIES those individuals which inhabit the colder and drier areas within its area of DISTRIBUTION are lighter in colour than those living in the warmer and wetter areas.

Gonad A sex ORGAN, part of the REPRODUCTIVE SYSTEM.

Gonys An angular part of the bill towards the tip of the lower MANDI-BLE, most noticeable in the gulls (FAMILY Laridae).

Gorget See BREAST BAND.

Graminivorous Feeding on grass. Geese (FAMILY Anatidae) are examples of graminivores (grazers).

Granivorous Feeding on grain or seeds. The finches (FAMILY Fringilli-dae) are examples of granivores.

Great Bustard Trust An organisation founded in 1970 to re-establish the Great Bustard *Otis tarda* as a British breeding SPECIES. In appropriate HABITAT, at Porton Down in Wiltshire, the Trust is rearing a captive stock which it is hoped will form a basis for INTRODUCTION into the wild.

Greater coverts See WING COVERTS.

Greater Snow Goose See LESSER SNOW GOOSE.

Grebe fur The soft TIPPET feathers of the Great Crested Grebe *Podiceps cristatus*, which were once in such great demand for the millinery trade that by the late nineteenth century the bird had become rare in the British Isles.

Greenland Falcon The SUBSPECIES of the Gyrfalcon *Falco rusticolus* breeding in Greenland. It has the SCIENTIFIC NAME *F.r. candicans*, and it is an irregular visitor to the British Isles in winter and spring. The race which breeds in Iceland, with the scientific name *F.r. islandus* (the 'Iceland Falcon') is a rare VAGRANT to the British Isles.

Greenland Redpoll See LESSER REDPOLL.

Greenland Wheatear The SUBSPECIES of the Wheatear *Oenanthe oenanthe* which breeds in Greenland and which appears in the British Isles on PASSAGE. Its full SCIENTIFIC NAME is *O.o. leucorrhoa*.

Greenland White-fronted Goose The SUBSPECIES of the White-fronted Goose *Anser albifrons* which breeds in Greenland and which winters mainly in Western Scotland and in Ireland. Its full SCIENTIFIC NAME is *A.a. flavirostris*.

Green-winged Teal The SUBSPECIES of the Teal *Anas crecca* breeding in North America. It has the SCIENTIFIC NAME *A.c. carolinensis*, the British breeding race being *A.c. crecca*. The green-winged race is a VAGRANT to the British Isles.

Grey goose A member of the GENUS *Anser*, part of the FAMILY Anatidae, for example the Greylag Goose *A. anser*.

Greyhen The female Black Grouse *Tetrao tetrix*, the male being the 'blackcock'.

Grid square A square of the National Grid as used on Ordnance Survey maps. On these maps 100 kilometre squares are designated by the use of two letters, 10 kilometre squares by a combination of two letters and two numbers, for example SK14, and one kilometre squares by a combination of two letters and four numbers, for example SK 1845. By quoting a six-figure reference, for example SK183457, the position of a point anywhere in Britain can be given to the nearest 100 metres. The grid square is being increasingly used in bird DISTRIBUTION surveys, rather than an administrative unit like a county or a VICE-COUNTY, whose boundaries are subject to change. In national surveys the 10 kilometre (10 × 10 km) squares are used, as in *The Atlas of Breeding Birds in Britain and Ireland* (compiled by the BRITISH TRUST FOR ORNITHOLOGY and the IRISH WILDBIRD CONSERVANCY), while local surveys often use the 2 kilometre (2 × 2 km) squares ('tetrads').

Ground colour The basic tint of an eggshell, masked to a varying degree by any markings present. For example, in the eggs of the Blackbird *Turdus merula* the ground colour is light blue but is more or less heavily obscured by reddish-brown spots and blotches.

Ground layer The lowest zone of vegetation, lying below the FIELD LAYER and consisting chiefly of mosses and lichens growing on the soil surface.

Ground speed See AIR SPEED.

Grouse moor See MOOR.

Guano A large accumulation of bird FAECES, properly referring to the thick deposit which may develop at a SEABIRD breeding COLONY in a region with a dry climate.

Gular Of the THROAT.

Gular pouch An extensible THROAT sac, used for short-term storage of food and seen, for example, in the Rook *Corvus frugilegus*.

Gullet See OESOPHAGUS.

Habitat The kind of place where an ORGANISM lives. Habitats can be classified at various scales, for example woodland or tree trunks, and can be divided and subdivided, for example, coniferous woodland, forestry plantations, pine forest or Scots pine stands. The term 'biotope' means more or less the same as 'habitat', although it tends to refer to the larger-scale habitats such as moorland or sea coast.

Habituation Development of a lack of response to situations and events which are found through experience to be harmless. Thus birds feeding in fields become habituated to farm livestock and those which use road verges come to ignore traffic.

Hallux The hind or 'first' toe of a bird. In a PERCHING BIRD it is well developed, but in one which runs on open ground it may be much reduced (or even absent) and raised above the level of the other toes, as for example in the plovers (FAMILY Charadriidae). In birds with TOTIPAL-MATE feet, the 'hind' toe actually points forward.

Hamulus See BARB.

Hand The section of the wing between the CARPAL JOINT and the tip. The bones concerned are the metacarpals and the PHALANGES. The hand carries the PRIMARY feathers and the ALULA.

Handbook A reference work covering the AVIFAUNA of a particular geographical area, giving as much information as possible for each SPECIES (in contrast to a FIELD GUIDE). The standard work for the British Isles remains *The Handbook of British Birds* by H. F. Witherby and others, which was first published in 1938–41 and is often known simply as 'The Handbook'. This five-volume work, however, is now being replaced by its seven-volume successor, *The Birds of the Western Palearctic*, edited by Stanley Cramp, K. E. L. Simmons and others, of which two volumes had been published by 1980. The wide area covered by the new handbook reflects the increasingly international outlook of British ornithologists.

Hardfowl Arctic-breeding duck (FAMILY Anatidae) which remain as far north as possible during winter, and so are best seen, in Britain, in northern Scotland. Examples are the King Eider *Somateria spectabilis* and the Long-tailed Duck *Clangula hyemalis*.

Hastings Rarities A series of RARITY records claimed for the Hastings district of Sussex between 1892 and 1930, but now considered as unacceptable because deceit is strongly suspected. A total of 594 such claims involving 16 SPECIES has been rejected as a result of research findings published in 1962 by E. M. Nicholson, I. J. Ferguson-Lees and J. A. Nelder.

Hawking Catching prey in the air. In one sense, 'hawking' is an alternative name for FALCONRY. Otherwise it refers to the capture of flying insects by birds, not only by the specialists such as the various kinds of AERIAL FEEDER but also by the opportunists, as when Starlings *Sturnus vulgaris* exploit a hatch of flying ants.

Hawk Trust An organisation founded in 1969 to encourage the study and CONSERVATION of all types of RAPTOR. The Trust is involved in research, protection schemes and captive breeding programmes. Its headquarters are at Loton Park in Shropshire.

Heath A lowland area dominated by heather, with scattered trees and bushes, notably gorse, and having an acid, infertile soil. Good examples are the sandy heaths of southern and eastern England (including the 'brecks' of south-west Norfolk and north-west Suffolk), although these have been much reduced by reclamation for agriculture and by afforestation with CONIFEROUS trees. Typical heathland breeding birds include the Meadow Pipit *Anthus pratensis* and the Yellowhammer *Emberiza citrinella*, while a few southern heaths still have breeding Dartford Warblers *Sylvia undata*.

Heat regulation See THERMOREGULATION.

Hedge Sparrow Formerly the standard name, now simply an alternative name, for the Dunnock *Prunella modularis*.

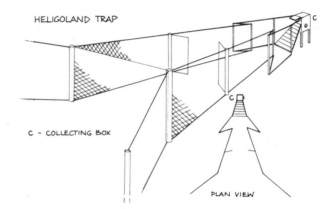

Heligoland trap A large permanently sited device for catching small birds for RINGING, consisting of a funnel-shaped structure of wire netting on a wooden framework, several metres across at its open end. Bushes may be situated in the mouth of the trap to tempt birds on MIGRATION to settle. The birds are driven into the narrow end of the trap where there is a 'catching box'. The Heligoland trap can be an important item of equipment for a BIRD OBSERVATORY, the one on the German island of Heligoland having provided the name.

Herbaceous Non-woody. Herbaceous plants, such as grasses and 'weeds', die down every year.

Herb layer See FIELD LAYER.

Herd A flock of swans (GENUS *Cygnus*).

Hesse's Rule   The contention that within a SPECIES an individual which breeds in a colder part of the area of DISTRIBUTION is likely to lay a larger CLUTCH than one breeding in a warmer part. This is possibly an ADAPTATION to higher egg loss and MORTALITY of young in an area of less favourable climate.

Hide   A structure which conceals the birdwatcher from the birds and so allows close observation. Hides vary from portable tents to permanent buildings provided at a NATURE RESERVE, and have observation slits or even glass windows. Hides may also be called 'blinds'.

Hill   See LEK.

Hindneck   The section of a bird's UPPERPARTS between the NAPE and the MANTLE.

Hind toe   See HALLUX.

Hippo   A member of the GENUS *Hippolais*, part of the FAMILY Sylviidae. This abbreviation for the SCIENTIFIC NAME of the genus is used mainly in RINGING and TWITCHING. There is no commonly found representative of the group in the British Isles, but the Icterine Warbler *H. icterina* is a scarce PASSAGE migrant.

Hippoboscid   See FEATHER LOUSE.

Hirundine   A member of the swallow FAMILY (Hirundinidae).

Histogram   A diagram showing a set of figures (values) divided into classes, each of which is represented on a graph by a bar or block (hence the alternative terms 'bar-chart', 'bar-graph' and 'block diagram'). A true histogram, as used in STATISTICAL work, shows the distribution of the values around an average, but the word is often used to refer to any kind of bar-chart, for example one showing the number of birds observed each month at a particular locality.

Holarctic (Region)   A ZOOGEOGRAPHICAL REGION which is actually a combination of two such regions, the PALEARCTIC and the Nearctic, thus covering the entire Northern Hemisphere north of the tropics. The concept of the Holarctic region can be a useful one because of the basic similarity between the AVIFAUNA of the Palearctic and that of the Nearctic.

Holm   See SKERRY.

Holotype   See TYPE.

Home range   The area over which an individual pair or group moves during the year, not to be confused with the 'range' (DISTRIBUTION) of the SPECIES as a whole.

Homing Pigeon   See FERAL PIGEON.

Homoiothermic or **homoiothermal**   See THERMOREGULATION.

Homologous Corresponding. The term is used particularly in comparative descriptions of the ANATOMY of different animals.

HOOD : BLACK-HEADED GULL.

Hood A mass of colour covering most or all of the head, as in the dark chocolate-brown example of the Black-headed Gull *Larus ridibundus* in breeding PLUMAGE. There is some overlap between the use of the terms hood and CAP.

Hooded Crow or **Hoodie** The SUBSPECIES of the Carrion Crow *Corvus corone* breeding in Ireland and north-west Scotland, and having PLUMAGE different from that of the more widespread race. The Hoodie has the SCIENTIFIC NAME *C.c. cornix,* while the other race is *C.c. corone.*

Hoodwink A possible RARITY which is not positively identified, usually because it is merely glimpsed, and which would probably prove to have been nothing out of the ordinary. The word was first used by the Scottish ornithologist Professor Maury Meiklejohn.

Hormone A 'messenger substance' produced by an ENDOCRINE GLAND with the purpose of stimulating an ORGAN into activity. The hormone-secreting glands are themselves activated by factors such as increasing length of daylight.

Horn See CREST and EAR TUFT.

Hornemann's Redpoll An alternative name for the Arctic Redpoll *Carduelis hornemanni.* Strictly it refers to the SUBSPECIES which breeds in Greenland, which has the SCIENTIFIC NAME *C.h. hornemanni,* the subspecies breeding in the Eurasian and North American Arctic being called Coues' Redpoll *C.h. exilipes.*

Host See DUPE and PARASITE.

Host-specific Living only on a particular type of host. The term is used of a PARASITE, many of which are confined to certain kinds of birds.

Hot searching See COLD SEARCHING.

Humerus The bone of the wing which is nearest to the body, corresponding to that of the upper ARM.

Hunger trace See FAULT BAR.

Hybridisation Interbreeding involving individuals of different SPECIES. Only related species can hybridise and hybrids tend to be incapable of reproduction. They are usually at a disadvantage in the struggle for survival as NATURAL SELECTION tends to operate against them. Therefore, hybridisation is undesirable and is seldom found in the wild among most groups of birds, various types of ISOLATING MECHANISM preventing mistakes being made.

Hypothesis A supposition based on observed fact. It can be tested by experiment or further observation followed by analysis of the data collected. Formulation and testing of hypotheses are fundamental in SCIENTIFIC enquiry. A hypothesis (or set of hypotheses) which amounts to a statement of basic principles becomes a 'theory', for example the theory of EVOLUTION by NATURAL SELECTION.

Hypothetical species A SPECIES which has been recorded in a particular geographical area, but whose occurrence there has not been substantiated by taking a specimen or a photograph. The development of modern optical aids and field identification techniques has enabled 'sight records' to become acceptable (provided an adequate description based on field notes is submitted to the appropriate RARITIES COMMITTEE), but the term 'hypothetical species' is still used in North America.

Iceland Falcon See GREENLAND FALCON.

Icterid A member of the FAMILY Icteridae, which contains the American or New World 'blackbirds' or 'orioles', unrelated either to the (Old World) Blackbird *Turdus merula* or to the (Old World) orioles (family Oriolidae). Two species of icterid have wandered to the British Isles, namely the Bobolink *Dolichonyx orizivorus* and the Northern Oriole *Icterus galbula*.

Immature A young bird in the first PLUMAGE after MOULT of its JUVENILE feathers. In many birds the immature plumage is very similar to that of the ADULT but in some, such as the Gannet *Sula bassana*, the immature passes through a whole series of plumages before reaching adulthood.

Imprinting The planting of a specific image in the mind of a newly hatched chick which it associates with parental care. Apart from its actual parent, humans or even inanimate objects can be imprinted on a young bird, provided they are the first things which it sees.

Incubation The warming of the egg by the parent bird, the heat being necessary for the development of the EMBRYO. In most birds which breed in the British Isles the BROOD PATCH is used for applying the warmth.

Incubation period   The length of time during which INCUBATION takes place, usually expressed in days. Birds may delay the start of incubation until the penultimate or the last egg is laid, thus ensuring that the eggs in a CLUTCH hatch more or less together. In cases where incubation begins with the first egg ASYNCHRONOUS HATCHING results.

Independent eyepiece focusing   See CENTRAL FOCUSING.

Indeterminate layer   See DETERMINATE LAYER.

Indigenous   Native to the geographical area under consideration. For example, the Grey Partridge *Perdix perdix* is indigenous in the British Isles, whereas the Red-legged Partridge *Alectoris rufa* is not, being an INTRODUCTION through human agency.

Indirect head scratching   Scratching the head by lowering the wing and then lifting the leg over the wing from behind, so that the head can be reached. 'Direct head-scratching', on the other hand, simply involves bringing the leg up to the head in front of the wing without the need for any movement of the latter. Each bird group characteristically uses one or the other of these methods, examples of those which scratch their heads indirectly being the nightjars (FAMILY Caprimulgidae), swifts (family Apodidae), kingfishers (family Alcedinidae) and most PASSERINE birds.

Individual distance   The gap between a bird and those around it, forming a 'mobile TERRITORY' into which other birds are not allowed, being warned off by aggressive postures. The principle of individual distance operates at all times unless it has been broken down by DISPLAY.

Ing   See FLASH.

Ingluvies   See CROP.

Injury-feigning   See DISTRACTION DISPLAY.

Innate   See INSTINCT.

Inner toe   The 'second' digit of a bird's foot, being the toe pointing towards the midline of the body. The 'first toe' is the HALLUX, which usually points backwards, the 'third toe' is the middle toe, which points more or less straight forwards, and the 'fourth' toe is the outer one, pointing away from the midline of the body. The arrangement is different in birds with SYNDACTYL(E), TOTIPALMATE and ZYGODACTYL(E) feet.

Insectivorous   Insect-eating. A large proportion of the birds found in the British Isles eat insects, and many are specialist insectivores, for example the various types of AERIAL FEEDER and the warblers (FAMILY Sylviidae).

Insight learning   Problem solving by evaluation rather than simply by trial and error. Some types of birds, notably the tits (FAMILY Paridae), show considerable ability in this respect.

Instinct The ability to act without the need for prior learning. Much of bird BEHAVIOUR seems to be instinctive or 'innate' but some has to be at least partly learnt, for example flying.

Institute of Terrestrial Ecology See NATURAL ENVIRONMENT RE-SEARCH COUNCIL.

Instrumental song The production of a sound which has the function of SONG but which is made by some means other than vocal. The best example is DRUMMING.

Interbreeding See HYBRIDISATION.

International Council for Bird Preservation An organisation founded in 1922 to promote the CONSERVATION of birds anywhere in the world. It has branches in participating countries and its headquarters are in Cambridge.

International Ornithological Congress An event which first took place in Vienna in 1884 and is held every four years in different locations, being an international SCIENTIFIC conference dealing with all aspects of ornithology. These meetings are organised by the International Ornithological Committee, and the proceedings of each are published. The seventeenth congress was held in West Berlin in 1978.

International Union for the Conservation of Nature and Natural Resources An organisation founded in 1948 to promote nature CONSERVATION anywhere in the world. Its headquarters are at Morges in Switzerland.

International Waterfowl Research Bureau An organisation founded in 1954 to promote and co-ordinate the study of WETLAND birds throughout the world. It was formerly called the 'International WILDFOWL Research Bureau' but is now concerned with all AQUATIC and RIPARIAN birds. Its headquarters are at the WILDFOWL TRUST at Slimbridge in Gloucestershire.

Interspecific Between two or more SPECIES.

Intertidal Between high and low water marks, or between tides.

Intestine The part of the ALIMENTARY SYSTEM between the GIZZARD and the CLOACA. It consists of a coiled tube which can be divided into two sections, namely the 'small intestine' (itself consisting of the 'duodenum' and the 'ileum') and the 'large intestine'. Digestion, absorption of water and formation of the FAECES take place in the intestines. In some birds, for example the grouse (FAMILY Tetraonidae), digestion is aided by the presence of two side tubes with dead ends, called 'caeca' (singular 'caecum').

Intraspecific Within a single SPECIES.

Introduction The establishment of a SPECIES by human agency in an area to which it is not INDIGENOUS, also called 'naturalisation'. It may result in the appearance of a FERAL population which can, ultimately, become truly wild, although many attempts at introduction have failed completely. Examples of species introduced to the British Isles are the Ruddy Duck *Oxyura jamaicensis* (an ESCAPE) and the Little Owl *Athene noctua* (a deliberate introduction). Many European species have been introduced elsewhere in the world.

Invasion   A rapid extension of the breeding DISTRIBUTION by natural means, being a form of COLONISATION. The most spectacular example in recent times has been the invasion of most of Europe by the Collared Dove *Streptopelia decaocto*, which until about 1930 was confined to the region from Yugoslavia eastwards. The term is also used for an IRRUPTION.

Iris (plural irides)   The coloured part of the eye surrounding the pupil and controlling the latter's size by expanding or contracting according to light intensity. The colours of irides in birds vary, being, for example, yellow in the Goldeneye *Bucephala clangula* and bluish in the Jackdaw *Corvus monedula*.

Irish Records Panel   See RARITIES COMMITTEE.

Irish Wildbird Conservancy   An organisation founded in 1968 to promote bird CONSERVATION and research in the Republic of Ireland, being the Irish equivalent of the BRITISH TRUST FOR ORNITHOLOGY and the ROYAL SOCIETY FOR THE PROTECTION OF BIRDS combined. It co-operates closely with British organisations and now publishes the annual journal 'Irish Birds'. IWC headquarters are at the Royal Irish Academy in Dublin.

Irridescent   Reflecting colours in bright light which are less obvious or even invisible in poor light. Irridescence results from feather structure, and occurs usually as a blue, purple or green gloss on dark PLUMAGE, notably on ducks (FAMILY Anatidae) and crows (family Corvidae).

Irruption   An irregular movement involving large numbers of birds which takes them into areas where they are not found every year in such numbers. An irruption differs from true MIGRATION because it is essentially irregular and does not have a return movement matching the outward movement. Shortage of food on the continent may cause irruptions into the British Isles involving birds such as Waxwings *Bombycilla garrulus* and tits (FAMILY Paridae) but the best known irruptive SPECIES is the Crossbill *Loxia curvirostra*. Irruptions into an area constitute 'eruptions' from the area of origin of the birds.

Isochronal line   A line drawn across a bird MIGRATION map joining up those places where arrival or departure dates for a particular SPECIES are the same, thus showing the progress of migration across the region concerned.

Isolating mechanism The means by which pairing is confined within a SPECIES, thus preventing HYBRIDISATION. Distinctive SPECIES-SPECIFIC features of PLUMAGE, CALL notes, SONG and DISPLAY are examples, these being particularly important where species are closely related.

Jess A leather strap used in FALCONRY, one end being attached to the bird's leg and the other to a steel swivel which, in turn, is fixed to a perch.

Jizz The overall impression which a bird gives an observer, enabling an experienced birdwatcher at least to suspect its identity, even if PLUMAGE details and other diagnostic features cannot be seen. Jizz consists of a combination of colour, size, shape and movement. The word was invented by the Cheshire ornithologist T. A. Coward.

Jugging The roosting of a covey of partridges (FAMILY Phasianidae), the group in the ROOST being called a 'jug'.

Juvenile A young bird in its first covering of feathers, which have replaced its initial DOWN. After a MOULT in its first autumn the bird may show PLUMAGE of an IMMATURE.

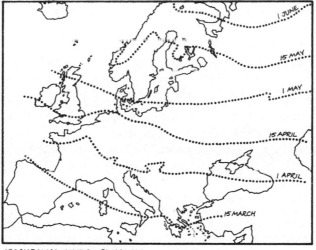

ISOCHRONAL LINES: SWALLOW

Keel   See STERNUM.

Keratin   A more or less horny substance present in the skin of all VERTEBRATE animals and, in birds, the material of feathers and the tough outer coatings of the bill, leg scales and claws.

Kleptoparasitism   The stealing of food by one SPECIES from another, also called 'piracy' or 'food-piracy'. The best examples of kleptoparasites found in the British Isles are the skuas (FAMILY Stercorariidae) and the gulls (family Laridae).

Knee   See TARSAL JOINT.

Lagoon   A shallow area of standing water. The term is most often applied to pools found on the coast behind shingle and dunes. These may be more or less SALINE and are attractive to most types of WADER and many WILDFOWL.

Lamella   A small thin plate of stiff hair, found for example lining the inside of the bill of the Shoveler *Anas clypeata*, and used in this instance to sieve small particles of food from the water surface.

Lanceolate(d)   Spear-shaped. The FLANK markings of the Fieldfare *Turdus pilaris* can be so described.

Larder   A collection of prey items impaled on thorns or barbed wire by a shrike (FAMILY Laniidae). Larders consist mainly of small birds and mammals, reptiles and invertebrates such as insects and worms; their occurrence is not confined to any particular season. Shrikes are sometimes known as 'butcher birds'.

Latin name   See SCIENTIFIC NAME.

Lead poisoning   A condition mainly found in WILDFOWL which have been feeding in areas contaminated with lead pellets. This can result from shooting or from fishermen discarding the weights from their lines, and the birds may swallow the pieces of lead either accidentally with their food or deliberately in mistake for grit. Mute Swans *Cygnus olor* are frequent victims on heavily-fished rivers.

Leaf warbler   A member of the GENUS Phylloscopus, part of the FAMILY Sylviidae. Common examples in the British Isles are the Chiffchaff *P. collybita* and the Willow Warbler *P. trochilus*.

Leap-frog migration   Autumn movement by the northern breeding element of a POPULATION to winter quarters which lie further to the south than those occupied by the southern breeding element of that population. Thus the northern birds 'leapfrog' over the southern birds, which may be

RESIDENT or move much shorter distances on MIGRATION than the northern birds. This situation is common among birds whose breeding DISTRIBUTION extends across both arctic and temperate latitudes. For example, in the Dunlin *Calidris alpina*, British breeders do not move far for the winter, whereas those from the Arctic migrate not only to the British Isles but also as far south as the Cape of Good Hope.

Leg flag   A brightly coloured ring with a broad flange, fitted to the leg so that the bird can be recognised as belonging to the marked POPULATION and its movements can be followed. Leg flags are usually employed only on relatively large birds.

Lek   An assembly of birds for the purposes of communal (or social) DISPLAY, originally referring to those of the Black Grouse *Tetrao tetrix* but now also applied to the similar gatherings of the Ruff *Philomachus pugnax*. On the display-ground ('arena' or, in the case of the Ruff, 'hill') the males defend small patches of ground called 'courts'.

Lesser coverts   See WING COVERTS.

Lesser Redpoll   The SUBSPECIES of the Redpoll *Carduelis flammea* breeding in the British Isles and central Europe, with the SCIENTIFIC NAME *C.f. cabaret*. Examples of the Mealy Redpoll *C.f. flammea*, which breeds in northern Eurasia and northern North America, and the Greenland Redpoll *C.f. rostrata*, also occur in the British Isles.

Lesser Snow Goose   One of the two SUBSPECIES of the Snow Goose *Anser caerulescens*. It has the SCIENTIFIC NAME *A.c. caerulescens*; the other subspecies is the 'Greater Snow Goose' *A.c. atlanticus*. The lesser race has two 'colour phases', a white one and a blue-grey one, the latter being called the 'Blue Goose'. These phases are not regarded as sub-species, but merely as examples of DIMORPHISM.

Leucism   See ALBINISM.

Life list   See LIFER.

Lifer   A SPECIES seen for the first time by a particular birdwatcher, who can thus place a new tick on his 'life list'. The term is part of the vocabulary of TWITCHING.

Light-gathering power   The ability of a pair of binoculars to pick up sufficient light for the object being viewed to be seen clearly, especially in poor light. It is also called the 'brightness factor'. For a given instrument this figure is obtained by dividing the diameter of the OBJECT GLASS (in millimetres) by the magnification, so that for a pair of 8×40 binoculars the value is $40 \div 8 = 5$. The higher this figure the more useful the instrument is likely to be for birdwatching, and those with a light-gathering power of less than four are generally not recommended. An alternative measure of performance is the TWILIGHT FACTOR.

Line transect   See TRANSECT.

Linnaeus   A Latinised version of the name of the great Swedish naturalist Carl von Linné, who invented the system of BINOMIAL NOMENCLATURE, as used in his book 'Historia Naturae', published in 1758. His system is still in use, although developments in TAXONOMY have led to many changes in the actual names used. The abbreviation 'Linn.' or 'L.', which is often to be found after the SCIENTIFIC NAME of a SPECIES, indicates that Linnaeus was the first author to describe and name the species.

Linnean Society (of London)   An organisation founded in 1788 and named after LINNAEUS, promoting the study of all aspects of BIOLOGY. Among its publications is a zoological journal. The society's headquarters are in London.

Lister   See TWITCHING.

Littoral   Of the shore. The term includes the INTERTIDAL zone and may also be used with regard to inland waters.

Loafing   Behaviour not connected with feeding or breeding. The term includes PREENING and resting and does not imply that time is being wasted. Some types of birds, such as WILDFOWL, have habitual 'loafing places'.

Lobate   Having lobes, as for example the foot of a Coot *Fulica atra*.

Local enhancement   See SOCIAL FACILITATION.

Local Nature Reserve   See NATURE RESERVE.

Lodge Pigeon   See FERAL PIGEON.

London Pigeon   See FERAL PIGEON.

Longevity   Length of life. For any given SPECIES in the wild, the actual life-span will usually be considerably shorter than its potential because bird MORTALITY is mostly caused by accident rather than old age. In captivity, of course, birds can be much longer-lived. In general, potential longevity is greater in large birds than in small ones. Gulls (FAMILY Laridae), for example, may live for over 30 years in the wild, whereas for a small PASSERINE bird half that figure would be very optimistic. In practice, relatively few of the birds hatched in a given BREEDING SEASON live for more than a few weeks.

Loomery   A breeding COLONY of Guillemots *Uria aalge*.

Loop migration   A type of movement which is similar to normal MIGRATION except that the return journey from the winter quarters to the breeding grounds follows a different route from that of the outward journey. For example, the White-fronted Goose *Anser albifrons* returns from its winter quarters in the British Isles to its breeding grounds in Arctic Russia by a route which lies considerably to the south of that followed in autumn.

Loose colony   See COLONY.

Lore   The region of a bird's exterior between the bill and the eye.

Louse fly   See FEATHER LOUSE.

Lumper   A scientist working in the field of TAXONOMY who tends to emphasise the similarities between SPECIES and group them together in the same GENUS wherever possible. The opposite kind of taxonomist is a 'splitter', who tends to emphasise the differences between species and to increase the number of genera. In modern taxonomy lumpers seem to outnumber splitters and many formerly separate genera are no longer accepted as such.

Machair   Grass-covered shell sand on the leeward side of dunes along the mainland coast and (especially) on the Hebridean islands of north-west Scotland. Typical breeding birds of the machair include the Ringed Plover *Charadrius hiaticula* and the Skylark *Alauda arvensis*.

Maintenance activity   See COMFORT MOVEMENT.

Malar region   The cheek, defined in birds as the area in front of, and slightly below, the eye.

Management plan   A scheme for maintaining a NATURE RESERVE so that the purpose of its establishment continues to be achieved. In practice management largely consists of the perpetuation of the required HABITAT range. For example, if open water is needed, encroachment by reed beds must be prevented, and the management plan will take such potential habitat changes into account. It is impossible to run a reserve properly without devising and implementing such a scheme.

Mandible   One of the two parts of a bird's bill (the upper and lower mandibles). They are bony outgrowths from the skull covered with horny sheaths of KERATIN.

Mantle   The upper part of a bird's back, lying between the NAPE and the part named the 'BACK'. The mantle forms a kind of SADDLE across the upperparts between the wings.

Marginal coverts   See WING COVERTS.

Marking   Making birds recognisable, either as individuals or as members of a particular POPULATION. Individual recognition is achieved by

RINGING, but the bird must be captured or found dead before the ring number can be read, unless the rings (and therefore the birds) are very large. Marking of birds by COLOUR DYEING or by the use of a LEG FLAG, NECK COLLAR or WING TAG enables an observer to recognise them as belonging to a defined population, but not as individuals.

Marsh   An area of waterlogged, well-vegetated ground with neither a continuous cover of water nor a peaty soil. If the water cover is continuous (but lack of open water prevents the names 'pond' or 'lake' being used), the area is called a 'swamp'. With a peaty soil, it is a 'fen' if the water is alkaline and a 'bog' if it is acid. A peat bog may be called a 'flow' in northern Scotland and a 'moss' in northern England. Typical birds of these types of WETLAND include the Snipe *Gallinago gallinago* and the Reed Bunting *Emberiza schoeniclus*.

Marsh cowboy   An irresponsible WILDFOWL shooter who may disregard the ethics of WILDFOWLING and the provisions of the bird PROTEC-TION LAWS. Marsh cowboys cannot be regarded as true wildfowlers and are usually simply young people fooling around with guns.

Marsh tern   A member of the GENUS *Chlidonias*, part of the FAMILY Sternidae. In the British Isles the only regularly occurring example is the Black Tern *C. niger*. Marsh terns are predominantly freshwater birds, while the other members of the family (mostly placed in the genus *Sterna*) are predominantly marine in the British Isles and so are referred to as 'sea terns' (for example the Common Tern *S. hirundo*).

MASK : GREAT GREY SHRIKE

Mask   A dark patch around the eye extending to the base of the bill, well seen in the Great Grey Shrike *Lanius excubitor*.

Mealworm   A type of beetle larva much used for feeding INSECTIVOR-OUS birds in the wild and in captivity. Robins *Erithacus rubecula*, for example, are very fond of mealworms.

Mealy Redpoll   See LESSER REDPOLL.

Mean   The average of a set of values (figures) calculated by summing them and then dividing the sum by the number of values. For example, the mean of the seven values 7, 4, 6, 7, 5, 7 and 6 is $42 \div 7 = 6$. If the figures are ranked in order (namely, 4, 5, 6, 6, 7, 7, 7) the middle value in the order, in this case 6, is called the 'median'. The figures one quarter and three quarters of the way along the rank are called the 'lower quartile' and 'upper quartile' (in this case 5 and 7) respectively. The value which occurs most often (7 in this example) is called the 'mode'. These terms are much used in the STATISTICAL analysis of QUANTITATIVE data on birds.

Median See MEAN.

Median coverts See WING COVERTS.

Median line or **median stripe** The middle line or zone of a section of PLUMAGE, such as the BACK or the CROWN. The Snipe *Gallinago gallinago*, for example, has a buff streak forming a median stripe on its crown.

Melanism Excess of black pigment (melanin) on the body, an ABERRANT condition producing darker individuals than normal.

Melogram See SONAGRAM.

Membrane A very thin flexible layer of TISSUE. There are many membranes in a bird's body, the most obvious one from the birdwatcher's point of view probably being the NICTITATING MEMBRANE.

Merse A type of SALTMARSH found on the Solway Firth, where it is particularly important for its flocks of wintering Barnacle Geese *Branta leucopsis*.

Metabolism The chemical balance within the body. The 'metabolic rate' is the speed at which chemical reactions take place; this rate is higher in birds than in mammals.

Metacarpal See HAND.

Mew Gull An alternative name for the Common Gull *Larus canus*.

Middle toe See INNER TOE.

Migration A regular seasonal movement of the whole or part of a POPULATION with an outward journey followed, some time later, by a return journey. Although most migratory movements involve travelling between breeding grounds and winter quarters at some distance, there are other types, including ALTITUDINAL MIGRATION and MOULT MIGRATION. An IRRUPTION or WEATHER MOVEMENT, because of its irregular nature, is not a true migration. The British Isles are well placed on a major FLYWAY and there is a well developed BIRD OBSERVATORY network for studying migration.

Migration watchpoint A place from which VISIBLE MIGRATION can be observed. Most such watchpoints are coastal, and the BIRD OBSERVATORY network is based on some of the best of them.

Migratory divide The boundary between two adjacent POPULATION groups whose autumn MIGRATION takes them in different directions. The divide may or may not be marked by a physical feature such as a mountain range. For example, for most SPECIES breeding on the Siberian TUNDRA there must be a zone west of which the population migrates south-westwards to winter in Europe and Africa and east of which there is a southerly or south-easterly movement to southern Asia, the East Indies and Australasia.

Migratory restlessness   The unsettled behaviour of birds immediately before they are due to depart on MIGRATION, also called 'pre-migratory restlessness' or (using a German term) 'zugunruhe'.

Mimetic   Mimicking sounds. For example, the SONG of the Starling *Sturnus vulgaris* is often mimetic, mimicking the notes of other birds and even mechanical noises.

MIRRORS : HERRING GULL

Mirror   A white spot on the otherwise black wing tip of certain SPECIES of gulls (FAMILY Laridae), for example the Herring Gull *Larus argentatus*. These mirrors are a basic identification feature.

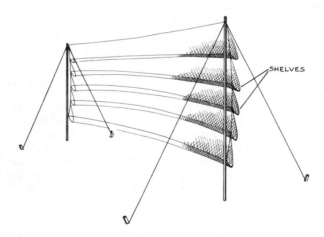

SHELVES

Mist net   A lightweight fine net mounted on poles and stretched across such a place as a woodland ride to catch small birds. The birds fly into the net, which is very difficult to see against a background of bushes and trees, and become entangled. Its portability and effectiveness account for the wide use of the mist net for catching birds for RINGING.

Mobbing The 'attacking' of a potential PREDATOR by small birds, usually in groups. Its function is presumably to confuse the predator. Not only genuine predators are mobbed but also some birds which have similar flight shapes to certain types of RAPTOR, such as the Grey Heron *Ardea cinerea* and the Cuckoo *Cuculus canorus*.

Mode See MEAN.

Model A representation of reality, either physical (as in a model bird used as a DECOY) or theoretical. In SCIENTIFIC research, a model, often mathematical, may be constructed to test a HYPOTHESIS.

Monocular vision See BINOCULAR VISION.

Monospecific Containing only one SPECIES. The term is used to describe a GENUS.

Monotypic Having only one form. The term is used to describe a SPECIES which has no SUBSPECIES, one which does have subspecies being called 'polytypic'.

Montane Of mountains. Examples of truly montane breeding birds of the British Isles are the Ptarmigan *Lagopus mutus* and the Dotterel *Charadrius morinellus*.

Moon watching Observation of the moon's disc in the hope of seeing birds on MIGRATION passing across it. Many small PASSERINE birds migrate at night, thus leaving the daylight hours free for feeding, and they are identifiable by their CALL notes as they pass over. Moon watching gives an indication of the numbers and directions involved in such migration.

Moor An area of open treeless upland, dominated by heather and having an acid soil, often waterlogged and peaty, a wetter part forming the type of MARSH called a 'bog'. Many moorlands are managed for the shooting of grouse (FAMILY Tetraonidae), and may be burned periodically to encourage the growth of young heather shoots as food for these birds. Moors are most extensive in Scotland, Wales, the Lake District and the Pennines. Apart from the Red Grouse *Lagopus lagopus*, their typical breeding birds include Curlew *Numenius arquata* and Meadow Pipit *Anthus pratensis*

Morph See DIMORPHISM and POLYMORPHISM.

Morphology The study of the shape or form of an ORGANISM.

Mortality Death, or the number of deaths. In the study of POPULATION DYNAMICS the 'mortality rate' is of great significance. High mortality of birds can result from an outbreak of disease such as BOTULISM, from adverse weather conditions such as frost or gales, and from man-made causes such as pollution or deliberate control.

Moss See MARSH.

Moult The shedding ('ecdysis') of old, worn feathers for replacement ('endysis') by newly grown ones. Most birds have one complete moult per year at the end of the BREEDING SEASON ('postnuptial moult'), but partial moults are commonplace, such as the 'prenuptial moult' before the breeding season. Most birds have the type called DESCENDANT MOULT.

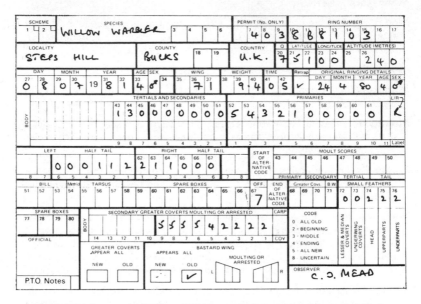

Moult card for an adult Willow Warbler replacing plumage, including flight feathers, before autumn migration

Moult card See MOULT ENQUIRY.

Moult Enquiry An annual survey organised by the BRITISH TRUST FOR ORNITHOLOGY in which people who handle birds (such as those involved in RINGING) record details of MOULT on special cards. These data increase knowledge of the timing and sequence of moult and its place in the lives of birds.

Moult migration A regular movement to and from an area where the birds MOULT. This type of MIGRATION takes place at the end of the BREEDING SEASON and is found in the Shelduck *Tadorna tadorna*, of which most breeders in the British Isles fly to the Heligoland Bight, with a smaller number travelling to Bridgwater Bay in Somerset. Presumably the purpose of such migrations is the provision of a safe moulting ground, especially as WILDFOWL become flightless during the moult.

Moult score The stage to which MOULT has advanced at the time when a bird is examined, expressed as a figure representing the sum of the degrees of growth of the new PRIMARY feathers, each scored from 0 to 5. As there are usually ten primaries, and only one wing is used in the calculation (the two wings undergoing moult simultaneously) the maximum moult score is 50.

Mounted specimen A stuffed SKIN set up for display in as lifelike a position as possible, usually with some indication of HABITAT around it. Although they are now mainly associated with museums, during Victorian times mounted specimens in glass cases were much in vogue as ornaments for private houses.

Mounting The male bird jumping or climbing on to the female's back for COPULATION. In order for the male's CLOACA to come into contact with the female's, she has to raise her rear while he lowers his.

Moustachial stripe A streak extending backwards and downwards from the base of the bill, above the MALAR REGION, as seen in the Bearded Tit *Panurus biarmicus* and the Reed Bunting *Emberiza schoeniclus*. This feature may also be called a 'whisker'. A similar streak immediately below it is called a 'sub-moustachial stripe', while a still lower one is a 'malar stripe'.

Mudflat An area of soft INTERTIDAL mud, not covered with vegetation. If it is invaded by plants, it becomes a SALTMARSH. In winter and at MIGRATION times mudflats may attract huge WILDFOWL and WADER flocks.

Mule A product of HYBRIDISATION. This term for a hybrid is used in AVICULTURE.

Multi-brooded See SINGLE-BROODED.

Mutant See MUTATION.

Mutation A naturally occurring GENETIC change leading to some individuals of a SPECIES acquiring characteristics which differ from those of other members of the species. If the mutant forms happen to have advantages which better equip them for survival, they will be favoured by NATURAL SELECTION and this might lead to SPECIATION. If, on the other hand, the mutants prove to be disadvantaged, in the course of EVOLUTION their characteristics will disappear from the POPULATION.

Nail A horny plate-like structure, shaped like a shield, found at the tip of the upper MANDIBLE of all SPECIES of WILDFOWL.

Nalospi The distance between the forward edge of a bird's nostril and the tip of the bill, a measurement being increasingly used in detailed QUANTITATIVE descriptions of birds.

Nape   The back of a bird's head between the CROWN and the HIND-NECK. The adjective, meaning 'of the nape', is 'nuchal'. The angle at the rear end of the head is called the 'occiput', for which the adjective is 'occipital'.

Nares   The nostrils. In all birds found in the British Isles these are placed towards the base of the upper MANDIBLE.

Narrow-front migration   See BROAD-FRONT MIGRATION.

Natal   At (the time of) birth.

Natal down   See DOWN.

National Nature Reserve   See NATURE RESERVE.

National Trust   The largest British CONSERVATION organisation, founded in 1895. Its purpose is the acquisition of areas of land and buildings which are of historical, architectural or SCIENTIFIC interest. Among the Trust's many NATURE RESERVE holdings are some of outstanding ornithological importance, such as the two north Norfolk reserves of Scolt Head Island and Blakeney Point. The Trust's headquarters are in London. There is a separate National Trust for Scotland, based in Edinburgh.

Natural Environment Research Council   A government body established in 1965 to promote and co-ordinate research into the physical landscape, plants and animals (the 'natural ENVIRONMENT'). It directs the research of its constituent organisations, such as the Institute of Terrestrial Ecology and the Biological Records Centre, which are involved directly and indirectly in a good deal of ornithological work, and gives grant aid to some private research bodies like the BRITISH TRUST FOR ORNITHOLOGY. NERC headquarters are in London.

Natural history   The study of all aspects of the natural world, with a tradition of field studies and amateur involvement.

Naturalisation   See INTRODUCTION.

Naturalists' Trust   A local society established to promote nature CONSERVATION in its area. These trusts are mainly organised on a county basis and some are known as 'nature conservation trusts' or 'trusts for nature conservation'. They deal with local conservation problems and some have considerable NATURE RESERVE holdings. The first example was the Norfolk Naturalists' Trust, founded in 1926, and the whole of the United Kingdom is now covered. The SOCIETY FOR THE PROMOTION OF NATURE CONSERVATION looks after the national interests of the trust movement as a whole.

Natural selection   The process by which those individuals which are best fitted for their ENVIRONMENT survive at the expense of those which are less well fitted. This helps the survival of the SPECIES as a whole, as those individuals which have disadvantageous characteristics are 'selected against'. Natural selection is a basic mechanism of EVOLUTION as it can lead to SPECIATION by favouring a MUTATION when it introduces particularly advantageous features.

Natural vegetation   The plant cover of a region occurring under natural conditions. In the British Isles man has destroyed or modified almost all the natural vegetation, which in most areas would consist of the type of BROAD-LEAVED woodland called 'DECIDUOUS summer forest'. Some of the typical birds of this vegetation type have adapted to the man-made ENVIRONMENT to become familiar suburban inhabitants, for example Robin *Erithacus rubecula* and Blackbird *Turdus merula*.

Nature Conservancy Council   The government body concerned with nature CONSERVATION in Britain, established in 1949 and orginally called the 'Nature Conservancy'. Its main activities are the acquisition of NATURE RESERVE land, giving grant aid to conservation organisations and monitoring the needs of nature conservation in general. Some of its nature reserves are of great ornithological importance, for example St Kilda in the Outer Hebrides and Caerlaverock on the Solway Firth. NCC headquarters are in London.

Nature conservation   See CONSERVATION.

Nature Conservation Trust   See NATURALISTS' TRUST.

Nature reserve   An area set aside to conserve aspects of the natural landscape, plants or animals. Such a place is subject to a MANAGEMENT PLAN so that particular types of HABITAT are conserved, rather than simply being left to run wild. Ownership and/or management of a reserve may lie with the central government (through the NATURE CONSERV-ANCY COUNCIL, which establishes 'national nature reserves'), a local authority (which establishes 'local nature reserves'), or a range of public or private bodies, notably the NATURALISTS' TRUST movement, the NATIONAL TRUST and the ROYAL SOCIETY FOR THE PROTECTION OF BIRDS. Public access to such reserves varies from unrestricted to non-existent, depending on their vulnerability to disturbance and the policy of their owners.

Nature trail   A route arranged so that a visitor to the area concerned can observe its most interesting features of natural landscape, plants and animals by reference either to notices or labels along the trail itself, or to markers which correspond to sections in a guide booklet. A wide variety of public and private landowners have organised nature trails.

Nearctic (Region)   See ZOOGEOGRAPHICAL REGION.

Near-passerine   See PASSERINE.

Nebbing   See BILLING.

Neck collar   A brightly coloured ring fitted round the neck so that the bird can be recognised as belonging to the marked POPULATION and its movements can be followed. The neck collar is a method of MARKING which is more suitable for large birds with long necks, such as geese (FAMILY Anatidae).

Nematode   See ENDOPARASITE.

Neossoptile   See DOWN.

Neotropical (Region)   See ZOOGEOGRAPHICAL REGION.

Nervous system   The network within the body which coordinates the activities of an animal and its responses to stimuli from its ENVIRONMENT. It operates by means of impulses travelling very rapidly along the nerves.

Nesting basket   A gourd-shaped wickerwork structure placed beside a piece of water for use by nesting ducks (FAMILY Anatidae).

Nest-invitation display   A part of COURTSHIP in which the male takes the female to a potential NEST SITE and 'invites' her to adopt it. This BEHAVIOUR is common among birds which breed in the British Isles.

Nest lining   The innermost layer of the nest. The eggs rest on the nest lining and it is usually made of finer material than the rest of the structure, feathers, hairs and soft plant parts being much used by smaller birds. The lining in the nest of the Song Thrush *Turdus philomelos* consists of pieces of rotted wood or dung stuck together with saliva.

Nest litter   The mass of loose material which builds up in the nests of birds with NIDICOLOUS young. It may consist of pieces of the NEST LINING mixed with DOWN, food remains and even unhatched eggs and dead young.

Nest platform   The fairly flat structure which comprises the nest for those birds which do not build a cup shape. Good examples are the nests of grebes (FAMILY Podicipedidae), which build floating platforms of AQUATIC vegetation anchored to reeds, tree roots and similar supports.

Nest Record Scheme   An annual survey organised by the BRITISH TRUST FOR ORNITHOLOGY and begun in 1939 as the 'Hatching and Fledging Enquiry'. Contributors complete special cards with such details as NEST SITE, number of eggs or young and eventual outcome.

Nest scrape   A small hollow excavated in soil, sand or shingle by a bird which does not make a 'proper' nest, although it may line the scrape with pieces of grass or similar material. Examples of birds which nest in scrapes include some types of WADER and the terns (FAMILY Sternidae).

Nest site   The actual spot at which a nest is built, as opposed to the geographical location. For example, a nest might be found at Minsmere in Suffolk, but the actual site could be in a reedbed or an oak tree, or on the open beach.

New World blackbird See ICTERID.

New World oriole See ICTERID.

New World sparrow A member of the group of birds within the bunting FAMILY (Emberizidae) generally called 'sparrows' in North America, although unrelated to the sparrows (family Passeridae) of the Old World. A few examples have wandered to the British Isles, such as the Fox Sparrow *Zonotrichia iliaca* and the Song Sparrow *Z. melodia*.

New World warbler A member of the FAMILY Parulidae, which is confined to North and South America except for wanderers, some of which, such as the Blackpoll Warbler *Dendroica striata*, have reached the British Isles. They are unrelated to the Old World warblers (family Sylviidae) and are sometimes called 'wood warblers', not to be confused with the Wood Warbler *Phylloscopus sibilatrix* of the Old World.

Niche The exact place filled by an ORGANISM in a particular ECO-SYSTEM, often called its 'ecological niche'. No two SPECIES can fill exactly the same niche, for otherwise one would be eliminated by NATURAL SELECTION.

NICTITATING MEMBRANE
LITTLE OWL

Nictitating membrane A transparent fold of skin, present in birds, which can be drawn across the eye to form a third eyelid. The function of this MEMBRANE is to clean the surface of the eye and protect it from dust particles and injury.

NIDICOLOUS CHICK

Nidicolous Hatching in a relatively undeveloped state and remaining in the nest for a period while completely dependent on parental care. Nidicolous (also called 'altricial') young are typical of birds which build substantial nests in well hidden or inaccessible places, notably all the PASSERINE groups, and they are naked, blind and completely helpless when first hatched. Young birds which are not nidicolous are NIDIFUGOUS.

NIDIFUGOUS CHICK

Nidifugous   Hatching in a relatively developed state and leaving the nest almost immediately. Although their parents may protect them and lead them to food, truly nidifugous young (also called 'precocial young' or 'downies') can walk and, in the case of AQUATIC birds, swim, right from hatching and are able to feed themselves. They are found in predominantly ground-nesting groups, such as WILDFOWL and GALLINACEOUS birds, while some other types, such as gulls (FAMILY Laridae) and terns (family Sternidae) have 'semi-precocial' young. Young which are not at all nidifugous are NIDICOLOUS.

Nocturnal   Active or occurring after dark. Apart from the owls (ORDER Strigiformes) there are no truly nocturnal SPECIES in the British Isles, although some birds feed a great deal at night, for example ducks (FAMILY Anatidae), and on MIGRATION many PASSERINE species move after dark. Otherwise British birds are active in daylight ('diurnal') or in a few cases CREPUSCULAR.

Nomenclature   A system of applying a SCIENTIFIC NAME to each ORGANISM or group of them. Only one system is used in SCIENTIFIC work, using BINOMIAL NOMENCLATURE for naming SPECIES and TRINOMIAL NOMENCLATURE for SUBSPECIES.

Nominate   See TRINOMIAL NOMENCLATURE.

Non-breeder   An individual which does not nest in a particular BREEDING SEASON, either because it is an IMMATURE, because it fails to establish a TERRITORY or to find a mate, or for some other reason. A bird which nests but does not manage to FLEDGE young is known as a 'failed breeder'.

Non-passerine   See PASSERINE.

Nonsense orientation   The tendency for certain SPECIES of birds to fly in a certain direction when released from temporary captivity, showing this ORIENTATION whatever the weather and time of day or year, and for no apparent reason. Mallards *Anas platyrhynchos*, for example, tend to fly north-west when released.

North Atlantic Gannet   See NORTHERN GANNET.

Northern Fulmar   A name used for the Fulmar *Fulmarus glacialis* of the Northern Hemisphere to distinguish it from its southern counterpart, the Silver-grey Fulmar *F. glaucoides*.

Northern Gannet   A name used for the Gannet *Sula bassana* of the Northern Hemisphere to distinguish it from its southern counterparts, the Cape Gannet *S. capensis* and the Australasian Gannet *S. serrator*. It may also be called the 'North Atlantic Gannet'.

North Sea Bird Club   An organisation founded in 1980 to take advantage of the opportunities for studying birds in the North Sea provided by the oil rigs. It is supported by several oil companies.

Nuchal   See NAPE.

Nuptial   Connected with breeding. Nuptial PLUMAGE is that worn during the BREEDING SEASON.

Object glass or **object lens**   The large lens of a pair of binoculars or a telescope. With 8 × 40 binoculars the magnification is eight times and the diameter of the object glass is 40 millimetres. The lens which is placed to the eye is part of the EYEPIECE.

Occiput   See NAPE.

Ocular   Of the eye.

Oesophagus   The tube along which food passes between the mouth and the stomach, also called the 'gullet'. It is part of the ALIMENTARY SYSTEM. Some birds, for example the various types of RAPTOR, have gullets which can greatly expand, thus enabling very large food items to be swallowed. The CROP is an extension of the oesophagus.

Oil gland   See PREEN GLAND.

Oiling   The spreading of oil over a bird's feathers, either during PREEN-ING or as a result of mineral oil fouling an AQUATIC bird after discharge, accidental or otherwise, into the sea or an inland water. Mineral oil causes the PLUMAGE to lose its insulating and waterproofing qualities, thus, in most cases, eventually killing the bird. Birds attempting to remove the oil with their bills often swallow lethal quantities of it. Oil pollution of coastal waters is becoming increasingly serious, affecting all types of SEABIRD, especially the auks (FAMILY Alcidae).

Old World warbler   See NEW WORLD WARBLER.

Olfactory   Connected with the sense of smell, which appears to be poorly developed in most birds.

Oligotrophic   See EUTROPHIC.

Omnivorous   Having a varied and unspecialised diet (literally 'all-eating'). Examples of omnivores, which are often 'opportunist feeders', are the gulls of the GENUS *Larus* and the Starling *Sturnus vulgaris*, whose success must, in part, be due to their adaptability in feeding.

Oology   The study of, and more specifically collection of, birds' eggs. Under the bird PROTECTION LAWS egg taking is now illegal with regard to most SPECIES of birds in the British Isles, as is the sale of the eggs of wild birds.

Open canopy   See CANOPY.

Open season   The time of year when a SPECIES which is legally recognised as a GAME BIRD may be shot. For the majority of such species the open season runs from August or September till January; the remainder of the year, during which the BREEDING CYCLE takes place, being the 'close season'.

Operation Seafarer   See SEABIRD GROUP.

Opportunist feeder   See OMNIVOROUS.

Orbit   The cavity in the skull which houses the eye. As sight is so important to birds, their eyes are large and in some types the orbits almost meet in the midline of the skull.

Orbital ring   See EYE RING.

Order   The division in TAXONOMY which lies between the CLASS and the FAMILY. The SCIENTIFIC NAME of an order always ends in '-iformes', for example the order Piciformes (woodpeckers).

Organ   A unit of the body which has a definite structure and function, for example the eye or the lung.

Organism   An individual plant or animal.

Organo-chlorine   A member of a group of chemicals used as pesticides in agriculture (for example DDT, BHC, aldrin, dieldrin and heptachlor) and also used in industry (polychlorinated-biphenyls or PCBs). The latter enter the ENVIRONMENT via effluents from factories. Birds can ingest TOXIC CHEMICAL residues by eating plants which have been treated with pesticides or by eating animals which have been contaminated by eating treated plants. Large doses can be lethal, while 'sub-lethal' quantities can cause various ill effects, notably reduction in BREEDING SUCCESS through such problems as EGGSHELL THINNING. These chemicals are particularly dangerous to birds which are at the top end of a FOOD CHAIN and some SPECIES of RAPTOR, for example the Peregrine *Falco peregrinus*, have suffered very serious population declines as a result.

Oriental (Region)   See ZOOGEOGRAPHICAL REGION.

Orientation   Direction finding during MIGRATION. Birds seem to have a 'sun-compass' which enables them to navigate by the sun or the stars and a 'biological clock' by which they can compensate for time of day, although the location and mechanisms of these capabilities are not known.

Ornithosis   A disease commonly found in birds, notably in pigeons (FAMILY Columbidae). It is also called 'psittacosis' because of its prevalence in members of the parrot family (Psittacidae). It is characterised by diarrhoea and rapid loss of weight.

Oscines   Members of a SUB-ORDER of the ORDER Passeriformes (PASSERINE birds) containing the 'songbirds', also called the Passeres. All the passerines found in the British Isles belong to this sub-order, the other three sub-orders of the Passeriformes not being represented.

Outer tail feather   A feather forming the side of the tail. In some birds these feathers are conspicuously white, for example the Pied Wagtail *Motacilla alba* and the Yellowhammer *Emberiza citrinella*.

Outer toe   See INNER TOE.

Ovary   The ORGAN which produces the egg. Female birds have two ovaries, one on each side of the body, but in almost all cases only the left-hand one is developed and functional. A working ovary resembles a very tiny bunch of grapes in appearance.

Ovate   Oval. The term is used in descriptions of birds' eggs.

Overbrooding   Continued INCUBATION of a CLUTCH of ADDLED eggs for a period longer than that required for normal eggs to hatch. This is quite a common phenomenon, the duration of overbrooding sometimes being absurdly long.

Overshooting   Movement beyond the normal limits of a bird's area of DISTRIBUTION by continuance in the usual direction of MIGRATION beyond the proper destination. By this means birds which are not normally found any further north than the Mediterranean region may reach the British Isles, for example the Black-eared Wheatear *Oenanthe hispanica* and the Subalpine Warbler *Sylvia cantillans*.

Oviduct   The tube which leads from the OVARY to the CLOACA in the female bird. The egg passses down it from the ovary, being fertilised and receiving its ALBUMEN and shell on the way.

Oviparous   Egg-laying.

Ovum   See REPRODUCTIVE SYSTEM.

Paddling   Trampling the surface of soft ground, also called 'foot-paddling'. This BEHAVIOUR is well seen in gulls (FAMILY Laridae), and it is thought that the vibrations encourage worms (which possibly mistake them for those caused by raindrops) to rise to the surface.

Pair bond   The mutual attachment between the members of a pair, maintained by DISPLAY and COPULATION.

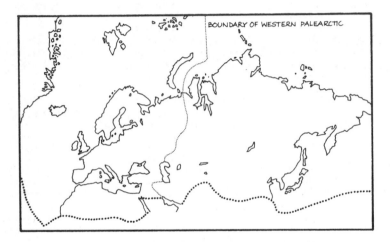

Map of the PALEARCTIC REGION

Palearctic (Region)   The ZOOGEOGRAPHICAL REGION which covers Europe, Asia (apart from the area south of the Himalayas and most of Arabia) and Africa south to the middle of the Sahara. In recent years it has been found desirable to define a 'sub-region' called the 'Western Palearctic', which, as used in the HANDBOOK *The Birds of the Western Palearctic*, consists of Europe (east to the Ural Mountains and the Ural River), the Near East and the Middle East (as far east as the Caspian Sea and the Persian Gulf, but excluding Iran and most of Arabia), North Africa (south to the mid-Sahara), the islands of the eastern North Atlantic, including Iceland, the British Isles, the Azores, the Canary Islands and the Cape Verde Islands, together with the European Arctic islands such as Spitsbergen, Franz Josef Land and Novaya Zemlya.

Pale-bellied Brent Goose   See DARK-BELLIED BRENT GOOSE.

Palmate(d)   Webbed.

Panic   A sudden and often unaccountable stir in a COLONY of such birds as terns (FAMILY Sternidae) in which the birds fly up and circle around. Usually the panic is short-lived and they soon settle down again. This phenomenon, especially if the birds are silent, may also be called a 'dread'.

Papilla   A small, brightly coloured, fleshy knob in the mouth of a NIDICOLOUS nestling, combining with the colours of the GAPE to guide the parent in placing the food which it brings to the nest. The number of papillae varies from one SPECIES to another and they are not present in all those with nidicolous young.

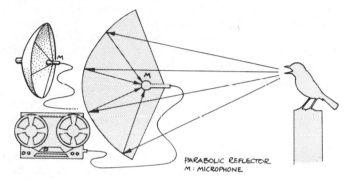

PARABOLIC REFLECTOR
M : MICROPHONE.

Parabolic reflector   An item of sound recording equipment in the shape of a bowl with a reversed microphone in the centre, much used in recording birds because it focuses sounds from the direction in which it is pointed and reduces extraneous noise like unwanted bird calls and the hum of traffic. A parabolic reflector microphone is connected to a tape recorder.

Parasite   An ORGANISM which entirely depends on another (its 'host') for its livelihood. An ECTOPARASITE lives outside its host's body, while an ENDOPARASITE lives inside. Birds suffer from a wide range of both types. In addition the Cuckoo *Cuculus canorus* is a BROOD PARASITE, while the skuas (FAMILY Stercorariidae) and the gulls (family Laridae) often practise KLEPTOPARASITISM.

Parson's nose   See PYGOSTYLE.

Partial migrant   A SPECIES in which some individuals are RESIDENT but others are involved in MIGRATION over varying distances. Many common species in the British Isles are partial migrants, for example the Meadow Pipit *Anthus pratensis*, which is partly a RESIDENT, partly a SUMMER VISITOR, partly a WINTER VISITOR and partly a PASSAGE migrant.

Passage   Movement through an area involving individuals which neither breed there nor spend the winter there, merely passing through on MIGRATION. As the British Isles lie on a major FLYWAY, very large numbers of passage migrants (also known as 'transients') travel through each spring and autumn. Some of these, such as the Little Stint *Calidris minuta* and the Spotted Redshank *Tringa erythropus*, are known in the British Isles only as passage migrants, but most SPECIES seen on passage have also RESIDENT, SUMMER VISITOR or WINTER VISITOR status.

Passeres   See OSCINES.

Passerine   A member of the very large ORDER Passeriformes, usually called 'perching birds' (literally 'sparrow-like' birds). Over half the world's birds are passerines and the order Passeriformes is divided into four sub-orders, of which the only one represented in the British Isles is the sub-order OSCINES. Those birds which are not placed in the order Passeriformes are called 'non-passerines', while those non-passerines which are most closely related to the passerines are called 'near-passerines', examples of the latter being the swifts (FAMILY Apodidae) and the woodpeckers (family Picidae).

Patagial tag   See WING TAG.

Patagium   The skin in which the bones and feathers of a bird's wing are embedded.

Peck order   See DOMINANCE.

Pecten   A thin ridge projecting from the RETINA of the eye and found only in birds. Its function is uncertain but it is largest in some types of RAPTOR and smallest in NOCTURNAL birds.

PECTINATE CLAW : BITTERN

Pectinate(d)   Comb-like. The claws of the middle toes of herons (FAMILY Ardeidae) are pectinated, presumably as an ADAPTATION for combing fish slime and scales from the PLUMAGE.

Pectoral   Of the breast.

Pectoral band   See BREAST BAND.

Pectoral girdle   The ring of bones which gives rigidity to the THORAX and provides support for the wings. The bones concerned are (on each side) the 'scapula' ('shoulder blade'), the 'coracoid' and the 'clavicle' ('collar bone'). The two clavicles are fused to form the 'furcula' ('wishbone').

Pectoral muscles The main flight muscles of a bird. They are necessarily massive, accounting for as much as a fifth of the bird's weight in the case of some pigeons (FAMILY Columbidae). They are anchored to the STERNUM.

Peep One of the smaller members of the GENUS *Calidris*, part of the FAMILY Scolopacidae. Examples of peeps are the Little Stint *C. minutus* and the Dunlin *C. alpina*. Originally a North American term, it is now widely used in the British Isles.

Peewit An alternative name for the Lapwing *Vanellus vanellus*.

Pelagic Of the ocean. A pelagic bird is one which, except when nesting, is found out at sea far from land, examples being the Fulmar *Fulmarus glacialis* and the Kittiwake *Rissa tridactyla*.

Pellet An object ejected by birds through their mouths, consisting of the indigestible parts of their food, such as bones, fur and the CHITINOUS parts of insects. Pellets are also called 'castings' and are said to be 'cast' by the birds concerned, which include INSECTIVOROUS as well as CARNIVOROUS types. Pellets are often used in the study of diet, although they may bias the results in favour of hard food items.

Pen A female swan (GENUS *Cygnus*), the male being the 'cob'.

Perching bird See PASSERINE.

Perching duck A member of the TRIBE Cairinini in the FAMILY Anatidae, these birds having the habit of perching on trees. The only British examples are the Wood Duck *Aix sponsa* and the Mandarin *A. galericulata*, and these are only present through INTRODUCTION by man.

Pesticide residue A quantity of a TOXIC CHEMICAL which may affect types of ORGANISM other than those pests for which it was intended. The most persistent such substances are those in the ORGANO-CHLORINE group.

Peterson Field Guide system The use of a pointer on a bird illustration to indicate a FIELD CHARACTER which is useful in identification. The device was used for a FIELD GUIDE in 1934 by the American ornithologist and artist Roger Tory Peterson and introduced into Britain in *A Field Guide to the Birds of Britain and Europe*, published in 1954.

Phalanx (plural **phalanges**) A section of a digit of the HAND or foot, namely a part of a finger or toe. In birds the fingers scarcely exist, and their phalanges are mainly fused. The foot, however, is usually well developed, with a HALLUX or 'hind toe' and the forward-pointing INNER TOE, middle toe and outer toe.

Phaneric See CRYPTIC.

Phase   See DIMORPHISM and POLYMORPHISM.

Pheasant Trust   An organisation founded in 1959 in order to conserve the pheasants (FAMILY Phasianidae) of the world, particularly those which are ENDANGERED SPECIES. A captive collection is maintained at the Trust's headquarters at Great Witchingham in Norfolk.

Phenology   The study of seasonal occurrences, such as the arrival of birds on MIGRATION and the start of the BREEDING SEASON, and their relationship with weather conditions.

Photoperiodism   The response of plants and animals to changes in the relative lengths of day and night. These affect the HORMONE producing glands and so control such aspects of the birds' lives as the timing of the start of the BREEDING SEASON.

Phyllosc   A member of the GENUS *Phylloscopus*, part of the FAMILY Sylviidae. This abbreviation for the SCIENTIFIC NAME of the genus is used mainly in RINGING and TWITCHING. The Chiffchaff *P. collybita* and the Willow Warbler *P. trochilus* are common representatives of the genus, a member of which may also be called a LEAF WARBLER.

Phylogenetic   Concerned with TAXONOMY.

Phylum   One of the basic divisions of the animal kingdom and the highest division in TAXONOMY. Birds, together with the other VERTEBRATE animals, are placed in the phylum Chordata, which contains all those animals which have a spinal cord.

Physiology   The study of the way the body works.

Pied Woodpecker   An alternative name for the Great Spotted Woodpecker *Dendrocopos major*.

Pigeon milk   A secretion from the CROP of members of the pigeon FAMILY (Columbidae) used for feeding the young and forming a milky fluid. Its proportion in the diet of the nestlings is reduced as they grow older.

Pin feather   A feather still confined within the horny sheath which protects it during the early stages of its growth and from which it eventually bursts forth.

Pinion   A flight feather, namely PRIMARY, SECONDARY or TERTIARY.

Pinioning   Depriving a bird of the power of flight by cutting a wing at the CARPAL JOINT. This is done while the bird is still young enough for the bones to be soft. Pinioned birds are never able to grow PRIMARY feathers on the wing concerned and so are permanently unable to fly. The birds most commonly pinioned are those in collections of captive WILDFOWL. Methods of producing temporary flightlessness include BRAILING and CLIPPING.

Piracy See KLEPTOPARASITISM.

Piscivorous Fish-eating. Apart from various AQUATIC birds, the Grey Heron *Ardea cinerea*, Osprey *Pandion haliaetus* and Kingfisher *Alcedo atthis* are piscivores.

Pishing See SQUEAKING

Plumbeous Lead-coloured, as in some of the greys in the PLUMAGE of pigeons (GENUS *Columba*).

Plumage The covering of feathers over a bird's body. It may vary with the age of the bird or the season of the year, and accordingly it may be described as breeding plumage, winter plumage, or JUVENILE, IMMATURE or ADULT plumage. In detailed descriptions of the external features (topography) of birds, standardised names are normally used for the various sections of the plumage, for example MALAR REGION and TAIL COVERTS. See diagram on page 117.

Plume A feather developed for the purposes of DISPLAY, being long and showy. Examples are found in the Great Crested Grebe *Podiceps cristatus* and the Ruff *Philomachus pugnax*.

Plumule See DOWN.

Plunge diving Dropping from a height into the water in order to catch fish. Although various PISCIVOROUS birds use this method of catching food, for example terns (FAMILY Sternidae) and the Kingfisher *Alcedo atthis*, the most spectacular plunge diving is seen in the Gannet *Sula bassana*.

PNEUMATIC. BONE (LONG SECTION)

Pneumatic bone A hollow bone filled with air, connected to the RESPIRATORY SYSTEM. Many of a bird's bones are pneumatic, with struts across their hollow interiors to provide a combination of light weight and strength as an adaptation to flying.

Poikilothermal or **poikilothermic** See THERMOREGULATION.

Pole trap An illegal and remarkably cruel trap mounted on the top of a pole. When any large bird lands on the pole the jaws snap shut, crushing the bird's legs. Despite the comparatively enlightened attitude towards animals which now prevails in the British Isles, and despite its cruelty and illegality, the pole trap is still widely used to destroy certain types of RAPTOR, which are themselves covered by the bird PROTECTION LAWS.

Polish Swan   A PHASE of the Mute Swan *Cygnus olor* in which the young birds are white instead of the usual grey, with pinkish or greyish feet instead of black. It is an example not of ALBINISM (as pigment is present in the eyes) but of 'leucism'. Polish Swans are rare in the British Isles.

Polyandry   See POLYGAMY.

Polygamy   Mating with more than one individual during a single breeding attempt. If a single male mates with more than one female the situation is called 'polygyny', an example of a polygynous SPECIES being the Corn Bunting *Miliaria calandra*. If a single female mates with more than one male, the situation is described as 'polyandry', an example of a polyandrous species being the Cuckoo *Cuculus canorus*. Most species, however, are not polygamous, although they may take different mates in successive years or, in the case of birds which are not SINGLE-BROODED, in successive breeding attempts within the same year.

Polygyny   See POLYGAMY.

Polymorphism   The existence of more than two distinctive forms (usually in terms of PLUMAGE) within a SPECIES. Each form, which is not regarded as a SUBSPECIES, is called a 'morph'. The males of the Ruff *Philomachus pugnax* are polymorphic, having a great variety of colour and pattern. Species with just two morphs are said to show DIMORPHISM.

Polytypic   See MONOTYPIC.

Population   A group of birds defined by the geographical area or the HABITAT in which they are found or by some other characteristic, for example unusual appearance as a result of a MARKING programme.

Population dynamics   The changing state of a POPULATION over a period of time. Studies of population dynamics of birds, often using data from such surveys as the COMMON BIRDS CENSUS, are important in identifying priorities for CONSERVATION efforts.

Population index   A measure of POPULATION level related to a base figure, usually 100. If the present index, for example, stands at 120 for a particular SPECIES, the population is now 20% higher than in the baseline year. This method of monitoring population change is used in the COMMON BIRDS CENSUS.

Porro-prism binoculars   A pair of binoculars in which the PRISMATIC arrangement is of the traditional type, in contrast to the more recently introduced ROOF-PRISM BINOCULARS.

Possible breeding   One of the three categories used in ATLASSING for recording the breeding STATUS of birds in a particular geographical area. It denotes a situation where birds are seen during the BREEDING SEASON in a suitable HABITAT for nesting but without any indication of breeding being observed. Evidence of 'probable breeding' (the second category) consists of COURTSHIP, or SONG heard more than once at the same place, or BEHAVIOUR suggesting the holding of TERRITORY or the presence of young. Discovery of a nest (in use or not long disused) or young, or observation of parental behaviour definitely indicating the presence of young, is evidence of 'confirmed breeding' (the third category). The sizes of the dots on the resulting DISTRIBUTION maps reflect these three categories.

Posterior See ANTERIOR.

Postnuptial After breeding.

Powder down A powdery substance into which certain tiny body feathers break down, found in members of the heron FAMILY (Ardeidae). Presumably it soaks up fish slime from the PLUMAGE. Other types of birds also produce powder from their feathers, for example pigeons (family Columbidae), 'powder impressions' of which may be left on windows into which they have accidentally flown.

Powder impression See POWDER DOWN.

Pre-adaptation The ability of a SPECIES to fit into a newly created HABITAT because its existing ADAPTATION pattern happens to be suitable. For example, the Great Crested Grebe *Podiceps cristatus* and the Little Ringed Plover *Charadrius dubius* were pre-adapted to the gravel pit habitat, and woodland birds such as the Robin *Erithacus rubecula* and Blackbird *Turdus merula*, were pre-adapted to the habitat of suburban gardens.

Precocial See NIDIFUGOUS.

Predator An animal which feeds on other animals, taking them as live prey. In practice, among birds, the term is chiefly used with reference to a RAPTOR, owl (ORDER Strigiformes) or some other CARNIVOROUS type, but INSECTIVOROUS kinds are, in fact, no less predatory than the carnivores. 'Predation' is the activity of predators.

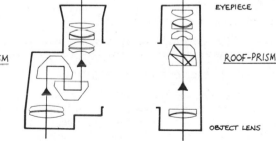

See PORRO-PRISM, opposite

Preen gland   See PREENING.

Preening   Running the bill along a feather in order to maintain it in good order. Disarrayed feathers are repaired by preening due to their BARB structure; preening also spreads oil over the PLUMAGE, secreted by the 'uropygial gland' or 'preen gland' situated just above the base of the tail. Constant preening is required if a bird is to keep its feathers in trim for efficient insulation and flight.

Premigratory restlessness   See MIGRATORY RESTLESSNESS.

Prenuptial   Before breeding.

Pricked   See WINGED.

Primary (feather)   One of the outer flight feathers ('remiges') of a bird's wing, used chiefly in manoeuvring. There are usually ten primaries and they are embedded in the skin of the bird's HAND. The SECONDARY and TERTIARY feathers, which are shorter than the primaries, form the other group of flight feathers.

Primary coverts   See WING COVERTS.

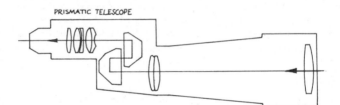

PRISMATIC TELESCOPE

Prismatic   Having prisms, namely angular pieces of glass which deflect rays of light. Prisms are used in binoculars and in some telescopes and their use reduces the bulk and weight of the instrument. There are two arrangements, producing PORRO-PRISM BINOCULARS and ROOF-PRISM BINOCULARS.

Probable breeding   See POSSIBLE BREEDING.

Productivity   The degree of breeding success. Productivity depends on the relationship between the 'reproductive rate' and the 'MORTALITY rate'.

Proof of breeding   See POSSIBLE BREEDING.

Protection Laws   The provisions of the Protection of Birds Act, 1954, and its later amendments. Basically all SPECIES of birds, together with their nests, eggs and young, are protected at all times in the United Kingdom, except for certain species regarded as agricultural pests and GAME BIRD species during the latter's OPEN SEASON. In addition vulnerable and rare breeders (those listed in the first part of the First Schedule of the Act) are protected by special penalties. Sale of the eggs of wild birds, even of common species, is illegal, as is the trapping of birds, except by authorised persons such as those licensed for RINGING. The ROYAL SOCIETY FOR THE PROTECTION OF BIRDS publishes material dealing with these laws and their enforcement. Similar regulations exist in the Republic of Ireland.

Protection of Birds Acts See PROTECTION LAWS.

Proximal See DISTAL.

Proximate factor See ULTIMATE FACTOR.

Psittacosis See ORNITHOSIS.

Pteryla See FEATHER TRACT.

Pterylosis The arrangement of the feathers on a bird's body.

Puffinosis A disease allied to ORNITHOSIS, sometimes causing heavy MORTALITY among young Manx Shearwaters *Puffinus puffinus*.

Pullus A nestling.

Pygostyle A plate-like bone forming the rear end of a bird's backbone and consisting of CAUDAL vertebrae fused together. The tail itself has no bones, comprising simply the tail feathers sprouting from a fleshy knob which covers the pygostyle and which is often called the 'parson's nose'.

Pyriform Pear-shaped. The term is used, somewhat inaccurately, to describe the shape of those eggs which are tapered towards one end, such as those of the WADER groups.

Quadrat A square sample of ground. A quadrat can be of any size, and this method of sampling can provide data, for example, on the density of plants or invertebrate animals per square metre, or on the bird POPULA-TION of a square kilometre (or GRID SQUARE).

Qualitative See QUANTITATIVE.

Quantitative Numerical. The increasing collection by birdwatchers of quantitative, as opposed to verbally expressed ('qualitative'), data is improving accuracy and objectivity and allowing a more SCIENTIFIC approach, often based on STATISTICAL analysis of the data.

Quarry species A legally defined GAME BIRD.

Quartering Methodically covering an area of ground, as might a hunting RAPTOR such as a harrier (GENUS *Circus*).

Quartile See MEAN.

Quill See RACHIS.

Race   See SUBSPECIES.

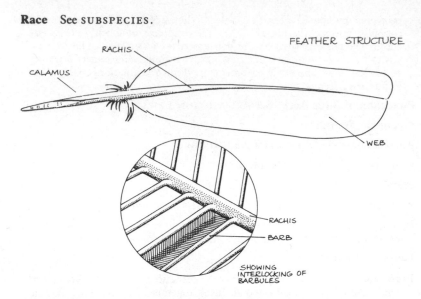

FEATHER STRUCTURE

RACHIS

CALAMUS

WEB

RACHIS

BARB

SHOWING INTERLOCKING OF BARBULES

Rachis   The stem of a feather, its lower end being buried in the skin. It is also known as the 'shaft', and its lower end, beyond the level of the lowest BARB, is called the 'calamus' or 'quill'. To either side of the rachis the WEB is attached. The term may also be spelt 'rhachis'.

Radar ornithology   Study of bird movements using the evidence shown on radar screens. Flocks of birds cause traces known as 'angels', which indicate MIGRATION across the area covered. Morning movements outwards from a communal ROOST such as might be occupied by Starlings *Sturnus vulgaris* form circular patterns called 'ring angels'.

Radius   One of the two bones of the middle part of the wing, corresponding to the forearm. The associated ARM bone is the 'ulna'.

Raft   A closely-packed flock of birds on water. The term is used mainly to refer to some types of SEABIRD and to ducks (FAMILY Anatidae).

Ramus   See BARB.

Range   See DISTRIBUTION.

Raptor(e)   A member of the ORDER Falconiformes, which contains the DIURNAL birds of prey, such as the hawks, harriers, eagles and falcons. The NOCTURNAL birds of prey are the owls (ORDER Strigiformes).

Raptor and Owl Research Register   An index of cards containing details of study projects concerned with any SPECIES of RAPTOR or owl (ORDER Strigiformes). Established in 1968, it is essentially an information service.

Rare bird   See RARITY.

Rare Birds Committee   See RARITIES COMMITTEE.

Rare Breeding Birds Panel   A five-member committee established in 1968 to document and report on the breeding of the 60 or so SPECIES defined as 'rare breeding birds' in the United Kingdom. It is financed jointly by the BRITISH TRUST FOR ORNITHOLOGY, the ROYAL SOCIETY FOR THE PROTECTION OF BIRDS and the journal BRITISH BIRDS, in whose pages the panel's annual report appears.

Rarities Committee   A body appointed to consider RARITY records and to decide if the identification of the SPECIES concerned is justified. Local committees deal with claimed sightings of species which are rare in their particular areas but not regarded as 'national' rarities, these bodies usually being appointed by local ornithological societies. The BIRD RECORDER usually receives records of rare birds for a given area, and submits them to the local committee or, if the species concerned is one of the 237 species defined as nationally rare, to the Rarities Committee of the journal 'British Birds'. This ten-member panel, often referred to as the 'Ten Rare Men', was established in 1959 to accept or reject rarity records of national significance, but is not the 'official' keeper of the BRITISH LIST, this being the function of the Records Committee of the BRITISH ORNITHO-LOGISTS' UNION. Therefore, if a record concerns a species new to the United Kingdom, the BRITISH BIRDS Rarities Committee sends it to the BOU Records Committee. Rare bird records for the Republic of Ireland are considered by the Irish Records Panel. In the case of both local and national rarities, full descriptive notes taken in the field at the time of the observation are essential for the acceptance of any record.

Rarity   A bird not normally seen in the area concerned but thought to have occurred there naturally (rather than as an ESCAPE). Each local ornithological society (or equivalent body) defines certain SPECIES as rare locally, while 237 species are listed as 'national' rare birds. Records of these birds must be submitted to the appropriate RARITIES COMMITTEE for verification if they are to be accepted as genuine.

Recovery   See RINGING RECOVERY.

Redhead   A female SAWBILL, not to be confused with the (North American) Redhead *Aythya americana* which has not been recorded in Europe.

Redirected attack   An onslaught by a RAPTOR, disturbed at its nest by a human or other large animal, on a passing bird rather than the intruder, presumably a kind of DISPLACEMENT ACTIVITY.

Red-spotted Bluethroat   The SUBSPECIES of the Bluethroat *Luscinia svecica* which breeds in northern Europe and northern Asia and which occurs regularly in the British Isles. Its SCIENTIFIC NAME is *L.s. svecica*. The 'White-spotted Bluethroat' is the subspecies which breeds in central and southern Europe east to Russia, and this too has occurred in the British Isles, though rarely. Its scientific name is *L.s. cyanecula*.

Reedling See BEARDED REEDLING.

Reeling Producing a continuous, monotonous TRILL, somewhat resembling the sound of a fishing reel, for example the SONG of the Grasshopper Warbler *Locustella naevia*. A rather similar sound is CHURRING.

Reeve The female Ruff *Philomachus pugnax*.

Register of Ornithological Sites The data collected during a survey organised between 1973 and 1977 by the BRITISH TRUST FOR ORNITHOLOGY to document those places in Britain which are important for birds. Its purpose is to provide a factual basis for advising planning authorities and landowners should any listed site become threatened by land use changes. The data consist of a description of each site together with a list of its birds, their approximate numbers and their use of the site for breeding or otherwise.

Regurgitation Ejection of partially digested food from the GIZZARD, mainly for feeding to young. It is well seen in the various SEABIRD groups.

Rehabilitation Return of a bird to the wild after treatment for injury, illness or OILING. Few seriously oiled birds can be rehabilitated, but, provided that proper care is available, fractures can often be successfully repaired.

Relative abundance The POPULATION of a particular bird SPECIES in a given area expressed as a percentage of the total bird population of the area.

Releaser A stimulus which causes an animal to react according to INSTINCT, merely triggering off a set response, known as a FIXED ACTION PATTERN.

Relict species A SPECIES which is thought to have been more widespread in the past but now, usually because of climatic change, has a discontinuous breeding DISTRIBUTION. For example, the Ring Ouzel *Turdus torquatus* is a relict species in southern Europe, where it is confined to high mountains, whereas further north it is more widespread. Presumably it was more generally distributed in the south during the cool period after the Ice Age, but as the climate became warmer it faced increasing competition from northward spreading species like its close relative the Blackbird *T. merula*, and was gradually forced out of the southern lowlands.

Remex (plural remiges) A flight feather. There are three types, namely PRIMARY, SECONDARY and TERTIARY feathers.

Remicle The outermost PRIMARY feather, very tiny compared with the others. This VESTIGIAL feather is not generally counted among the ten 'normal' primaries and is usually hidden by them.

Remiges See REMEX.

Replacement A CLUTCH laid to replace one which has been removed from the nest by a PREDATOR.

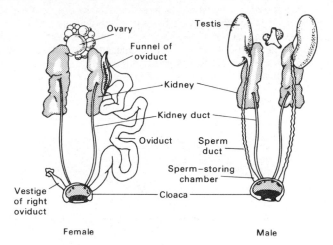

Female

Male

Reproductive system The parts of the body concerned with the production of sperms (spermatozoa) in the male and eggs (ova) in the female. A reproductive ORGAN is called a 'gonad'. The system consists essentially of the male's 'testes' and the female's OVARY.

Resident A SPECIES of which examples can be found in a particular area at any time of the year, although they may not be the same individuals, as few birds are completely SEDENTARY. Mostly, a resident species will also be a PARTIAL MIGRANT, either a SUMMER VISITOR, WINTER VISITOR or PASSAGE MIGRANT, or even all of these, as in the case of the Lapwing *Vanellus vanellus* or the Linnet *Carduelis cannabina*. Examples of species which are almost entirely resident are the Wren *Troglodytes troglodytes* and the Bullfinch *Pyrrhula pyrrhula*.

Respiratory system The lungs and associated structures, whose function is to extract oxygen from the air and to remove carbon dioxide from the body. In birds, because of their inability to sweat, the respiratory system is also important in THERMOREGULATION. The AIR SAC and the PNEUMATIC BONE are special features resulting from the ADAPTATION of bird bodies for flight.

Reticulate(d) See SCUTELLATE(D).

Retina The light-sensitive layer lining the inside of the eyeball. It is made up of 'rods' and 'cones', the former being most numerous in NOCTUR-NAL birds, the latter in DIURNAL birds.

Retrap   See RINGING RECOVERY.

Retrix (plural retrices)   A tail feather.

Reverse migration   A phenomenon in which birds fly in a direction opposite to that which they would be expected to take during a particular MIGRATION. It is possibly caused by INSTINCT causing an inappropriate reaction to some factor of the ENVIRONMENT. Reversed migration may bring to the British Isles in autumn migrants from eastern Europe which should have flown south-eastwards, for example the Arctic Warbler *Phylloscopus borealis* and the Red-breasted Flycatcher *Ficedula parva*.

Rhachis   See RACHIS.

RICTAL BRISTLES : SPOTTED FLYCATCHER

Rictal bristle   One of a group of stiff, hair-like feathers around the base of the bill. They are well seen in INSECTIVOROUS birds, perhaps helping to secure struggling prey after initial capture.

Ring angel   See RADAR ORNITHOLOGY.

Ringed Guillemot   See BRIDLED GUILLEMOT.

Ringing   MARKING a bird by placing a ring on its leg. Although CLOSE RINGING is practised in AVICULTURE, and plastic rings are used in research projects where COLOUR RINGING is necessary, most rings used for wild birds consist of thin strips of a very lightweight alloy (aluminium for small birds and nickel for larger ones) and are pressed round the leg with RINGING PLIERS. Each ring is numbered and carries the address of the RINGING SCHEME concerned. In the case of a RINGING RECOVERY the bird's movement can be traced, and thus ringing makes a valuable contribution to the study of MIGRATION and DISTRIBUTION. Length of time between ringing and recovery gives an indication of LONGEVITY, and while the bird is in the hand it can be weighed, measured and otherwise closely examined. Ringing is strictly controlled under the bird PROTECTION LAWS, both a RINGING PERMIT and a licence being required to practise it.

Ringing group   A number of enthusiasts who meet regularly for bird RINGING sessions. Such groups are organised with varying degrees of formality, and usually concentrate their efforts on particular places and/or particular types of birds. A well known example is the Wash WADER Ringing Group.

Ringing licence   See RINGING PERMIT.

Ringing permit   Authorisation for RINGING birds, being a legal requirement in the British Isles. Such permits are issued by the BRITISH TRUST FOR ORNITHOLOGY to those who have undergone the necessary training, which is both rigorous and lengthy. In addition a ringing licence is required from the NATURE CONSERVANCY COUNCIL, (or, as appropriate, from the Manx government, Northern Ireland Department of the Environment or Irish Forest and Wildlife Service), as under the bird PROTECTION LAWS it is illegal to catch most SPECIES of birds without such permission.

Ringing pliers   An instrument for closing a ring around a bird's leg, being a pair of pliers which when closed has circular gaps, each corresponding to a particular size of ring.

Ringing recovery   A ringed bird killed or found dead and reported to the RINGING authorities in the country where the bird was ringed. If it is caught alive by a ringer, the details on the ring noted and the bird subsequently released, it is said to be a 'control'. If the bird is caught soon after ringing at the same place where it was ringed, it is called a 'retrap'.

Ringing scheme   The organisation and administration of RINGING in a particular country. The British scheme, founded in 1909 by H. F. Witherby in association with his journal BRITISH BIRDS, has been the responsibility of the BRITISH TRUST FOR ORNITHOLOGY since 1937. The address given on most British rings, however, is 'British Museum (Nat. Hist.), London SW7', which is thought likely to mean more to foreigners than the address of the BTO headquarters. The British scheme also covers the whole of Ireland, and is a member of the European organisation EURING.

Ringing station   A place where regular RINGING of birds is carried out. It may have permanent facilities, as at a BIRD OBSERVATORY, or it may be manned by mobile ringers with portable nets or traps. A RINGING GROUP is likely to operate one or more such stations.

Ring species   A SPECIES which has gradually expanded its breeding DISTRIBUTION from its point of origin right round the world at the latitudes concerned until the two ends of its ring-like range meet. Each stage of the expansion has involved slight changes in the birds' characteristics, so that by the time the two ends of the ring join and overlap the two stocks are sufficiently different for them not to interbreed or, in other words, SPECIATION has taken place. The Lesser Black-backed Gull *Larus fuscus* and the Herring Gull *L. argentatus* are thought to represent the two ends of such a ring, the British Isles being in the area where they overlap.

Ringtail   A female Hen Harrier *Circus cyaneus* or a female Montagu's Harrier *C. pygargus*.

Riparian   Living or situated on the banks of inland waters. The Kingfisher *Alcedo atthis* and Sand Martin *Riparia riparia* are examples of riparian breeders.

Ritualisation   The development of DISPLAY. Simple actions, such as those involved in feeding or PREENING, have become ritualised into display patterns in which the functions of the original actions play no part.

Rocket net   A net attached to rockets fired over a flock of birds feeding on the ground. A 'cannon net' works on a similar principle but uses guns instead of rockets. These nets are chiefly used for catching geese (FAMILY Anatidae) in winter and have been developed by the WILD-FOWL TRUST for this purpose.

Rodent run   The practice of fleeing from a potential PREDATOR by crouching and running with head down through ground vegetation, an action suggesting a mammal rather than a bird. The rodent run is characteristic of ground-living groups such as the GALLINACEOUS birds.

Roding   The owl-like flight of the Woodcock *Scolopax rusticola* in which the bird flies over a more or less regular course giving two types of CALL, a low croak and a fairly high 'tsiwick'. This performance takes place in the dusk, as the Woodcock is CREPUSCULAR. It presumably has some significance in COURTSHIP.

Roof-prism binoculars   An instrument with an arrangement of its prisms which greatly reduces weight and bulk, thus recommending good quality examples of this type to birdwatchers. They may also be called 'Dialyt-type' binoculars after the trade name which the Carl Zeiss company uses for its roof-prism range. Instruments which have the traditional PRISMA-TIC arrangement are called PORRO-PRISM BINOCULARS. See page 91.

Rookooing   The production of a bubbling sound by the male Black Grouse *Tetrao tetrix* at the LEK. It is a kind of SONG.

Roost   A place where birds sleep, as opposed to a mere LOAFING ground. As most SPECIES are active during daylight ('diurnal'), they occupy their roosts during the night, but NOCTURNAL birds have daytime roosts and those birds whose activities are governed by tides, for example some WILDFOWL and WADER species, have high-tide roosts at any hour. A roost can contain any number of birds from one to several million, and may be situated on water, on the ground, in low vegetation, in bushes or trees, or on buildings or other man-made structures. Among the most obvious roosts are those of gulls (FAMILY Laridae) on lakes and reservoirs and of Starlings *Sturnus vulgaris* in small woods and on city buildings. The birds may FLIGHT to such roosts from considerable distances.

Rostral   Of the bill ('rostrum').

Royal Society for the Protection of Birds   The largest British ornithological organisation, founded in 1889 and concerned with the CONSERVATION of the birds of the United Kingdom. To this end it evaluates and takes action against the various threats to birds, helps the police to enforce the PROTECTION LAWS, has an active programme of NATURE RESERVE acquisition and management and educates the general public about birds and their conservation. Its junior section is the YOUNG ORNITHOLOGISTS' CLUB. The RSPB publishes the quarterly magazine 'Birds', which has the largest circulation of any British periodical on NATURAL HISTORY. Its headquarters are at Sandy in Bedfordshire and it has several regional offices and many local members' groups. The IRISH WILDBIRD CONSERVANCY is the corresponding organisation in the Republic of Ireland.

RUFF

Ruff   A ring of long and mainly brightly coloured feathers forming a very wide collar, best seen in the male Ruff *Philomachus pugnax* in breeding PLUMAGE.

Rump   The section of a bird's upperparts immediately above the upper TAIL COVERTS. It is often conspicuously coloured and so can be an important identification feature, for example in some types of WADER. The rump is also called the 'uropygium'.

Runt   A chick which is noticeably smaller and less developed than the others in its brood. Runting is an abnormality in most types of birds, although differently-sized young are found quite normally in those which have ASYNCHRONOUS HATCHING.

Rush   A FALL of birds on MIGRATION, or a succession of RARITY sightings.

SADDLE : GREAT BLACK BACKED GULL

Saddle   The MANTLE of a gull (FAMILY Laridae) or a similarly-shaped bird. The term is used where the colour of the upper surface of the wings continues across the mantle without a break.

Sahel Zone   The belt of grassland with trees ('savanna') and thorny scrub which lies immediately south of the Sahara. Several SPECIES of SUMMER VISITOR to the British Isles winter in the Sahel, which is subject to drought. The population crash of the Whitethroat *Sylvia communis* in 1969 may have been caused by such a drought.

Saline   Having a high salt content. The term is frequently used in describing water and soil. If the salinity is less but still appreciable, water may be described as 'brackish'.

Salt gland   A GLAND situated just above the eye of a bird, extracting salt from its body and expelling it as a strong solution through the nostrils (a form of EXCRETION). These glands are particularly useful for marine birds, which are thus enabled to drink seawater.

Salting or **saltmarsh**   An area of INTERTIDAL mud which has been colonised by salt-adapted ('halophytic') plants such as glasswort (*Salicornia*) and seablite (*Suaeda*). Saltmarshes typically have a branching network of muddy creeks. They are particularly attractive to DABBLING DUCK and many types of WADER.

Sanctuary Order   See BIRD SANCTUARY.

Sawbill   A DIVING DUCK of the GENUS *Mergus*, part of the FAMILY Anatidae. Sawbills have serrated cutting edges on their bills, an ADAPTATION for catching and holding fish, their main food. The common sawbills of the British Isles are the Red-breasted Merganser *M. serrator* and the Goosander *M. merganser*.

Scapula   See PECTORAL GIRDLE.

Scapular (feather) One of the feathers which cover the shoulder of a bird, namely the area where the upperwing joins the body.

Schedule One Species See PROTECTION LAWS.

Scientific In accordance with the philosophy and methods of science, which attempts to collect, classify and explain those facts which are expressions of the operation of natural laws. In academic terms ornithology forms part of the science of ZOOLOGY. Scientific method emphasises accuracy and objectivity, hence the importance of the collection of QUANTITATIVE data and its STATISTICAL analysis in scientific research on birds.

Scientific name An internationally agreed and understood label which has been officially attached to each division recognised in TAXONOMY. Although often called 'Latin names', many of them are not derived from Latin at all. There are strict conventions regarding the use of these names so that there is complete uniformity in the way they are applied. Their purpose is to avoid the confusion and language difficulties inherent in the use of common or 'vernacular' names. The application of SCIENTIFIC names is known as NOMENCLATURE.

Scottish Field Studies Association See FIELD STUDIES COUNCIL.

Scottish Ornithologists' Club The ornithological organisation for Scotland, founded in 1936. It publishes the quarterly journal 'Scottish Birds' and the annual 'Scottish Bird Report'. Its headquarters are in Edinburgh.

Scrape A shallow water-filled hollow excavated at a NATURE RESERVE in order to attract water birds, particularly various types of WADER. The original example was 'The Scrape' at Minsmere in Suffolk, a reserve of the ROYAL SOCIETY FOR THE PROTECTION OF BIRDS. The term is also used with reference to a NEST SCRAPE.

Scrub Bushes and small trees, forming the SHRUB LAYER. If it replaces felled woodland, scrub may be called 'secondary growth'. Typical scrubland birds are the Dunnock *Prunella modularis* and the Blackbird *Turdus merula*. The similarity (for a bird) of scrub to shrubberies in gardens has allowed such SPECIES to colonise suburban areas.

SAWBILL : GOOSANDER

Scute   See SCUTELLATE(D).

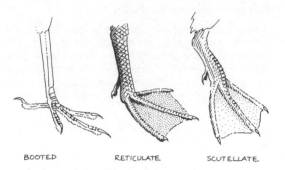

BOOTED   RETICULATE   SCUTELLATE

Scutellate(d)   Shield-shaped. The term is used in describing the pattern of leg scales on birds where these form 'scutes', namely shield-like overlapping structures as found in the ducks (FAMILY Anatidae). Where the scales do not overlap the pattern is described as 'reticulate(d)' ('netlike'), as found in the swans (GENUS Cygnus). In cases where no scales are present, the legs being covered by a continuous skin, for example in the thrushes (FAMILY Turdidae), the term 'booted' is used.

Seabird   Theoretically any SPECIES which has a marine HABITAT. In practice the term usually refers to specific bird groups, not all the members of which are truly marine, and some exclusively marine birds are not included, for example the Eider *Somateria mollissima*. The groups usually regarded as 'seabirds' comprise the ORDER Procellariiformes (petrels and shearwaters), the order Pelecaniformes (the Gannet *Sula bassana* and cormorants), the FAMILY Stercorariidae (skuas), the family Laridae (gulls), the family Sternidae (terns) and the family Alcidae (auks). All these families are placed in the order Charadriiformes, which also contains the various WADER groups.

Seabird Group   An organisation founded in 1966 for SEABIRD study. Its best known work to date has been 'Operation Seafarer', a POPULATION survey of British and Irish seabirds carried out in 1969 and 1970.

Sea duck   A duck (FAMILY Anatidae) associated to a greater or lesser extent with a marine rather than a freshwater HABITAT. Some of these are called 'bay ducks' in North America. The Eider *Somateria mollissima* is the only example occurring commonly in the British Isles which is marine throughout the year, but a number of others, such as the Scaup *Aythya marila*, the Long-tailed Duck *Clangula hyemalis* and the scoters (GENUS *Melanitta*) spend the winter mainly on the sea. The Shelduck *Tadorna tadorna* and the Wigeon *Anas penelope*, although much associated with coasts, are more characteristic of ESTUARY or SALTMARSH habitats than the sea itself and so would not normally be called 'sea ducks'.

Sea Eagle An alternative name for the White-tailed Eagle *Haliaeetus albicilla*.

Seagull Any kind of gull (FAMILY Laridae). The term is not used by birdwatchers, as many gulls are not even coastal, far less marine.

Search image The mental image which a bird develops with regard to suitable HABITAT, food and NEST SITE, thus enabling it to meet its various needs.

Sea tern See MARSH TERN.

Sea watching The practice of carefully scanning the sea with binoculars or a telescope to spot birds on the water or flying past well out from shore, either to look for a RARITY or to count the commoner birds. Good seawatching points are promontories such as Portland Bill (Dorset) and Flamborough Head (North Humberside).

Secondary (feather) One of the inner flight feathers ('remiges') of a bird's wing, between the PRIMARY and TERTIARY feathers. The secondaries vary in number from nine to twenty, according to the type of bird, and they are embedded in the skin of the bird's 'forearm'. Their chief use is in propulsion.

Secondary coverts See WING COVERTS.

Secondary growth See SCRUB.

Secondary sexual character A point of difference between the sexes within a particular SPECIES, other than the primary difference in the REPRODUCTIVE SYSTEM. Examples are the black plumage of the male and the brown plumage of the female in the Blackbird *Turdus merula*.

Secretion A substance produced by a GLAND, or the movement of such a substance from the inside to the outside of a gland. Among the more important are the various HORMONE secretions.

Sedentary Not moving far at any time. There are few truly sedentary birds in the British Isles, although many SPECIES are described as RESIDENT. Examples of species in which the majority of individuals are sedentary are the Dipper *Cinclus cinclus* and the House Sparrow *Passer domesticus*.

Semi-colonial See COLONY.

AVOCET

Semi-palmate(d) Half-webbed, as in the foot of the Avocet *Recurvirostra avosetta*.

Semiplume   A feather intermediate in type between a CONTOUR FEATHER and DOWN.

Semi-precocial   See NIDIFUGOUS.

Seral   Concerning the progressive re-establishment of the NATURAL VEGETATION of an area after its removal or destruction. Each seral COMMUNITY or 'sere' is one of a 'succession' which culminates in the 'climax' (the vegetation which the climate of the area favours most, namely its 'natural vegetation'). In most parts of the British Isles the seral sequence would consist of HERBACEOUS plants followed by SCRUB leading to a woodland climax, each having a bird POPULATION suited to the HABITAT which it provides.

Set   An alternative term for a CLUTCH.

Sexual dimorphism   See DIMORPHISM.

Shaft   See RACHIS.

Shank   See TARSUS.

Sharming   The production of a strange combination of grunts and squeals by the Water Rail *Rallus aquaticus*, particularly when involved in disputes over feeding areas.

Shearing   Tipping from one side to the other in GLIDING flight, so that when flying over water first one wing tip, then the other, appears almost to touch the surface. This habit has given shearwaters (FAMILY Procellariidae) their name.

Sheldgoose   One of the larger members of the TRIBE Tadornini (which also contains the shelducks) in the FAMILY Anatidae. The only example found in the British Isles is the Egyptian Goose *Alopochen aegyptiacus*, an INTRODUCTION to England.

Shorebird   The North American term for WADER.

Shrub layer   The zone of vegetation which lies below the TREE LAYER and above the FIELD LAYER, up to a height of about eight metres. It consists of bushes and small trees and in woodland it may be called the 'understorey'. Where no tree layer is present the shrub layer forms SCRUB.

Shunting   Moving fitfully along a coastline instead of striking out over the sea. Birds on autumn MIGRATION, for example, may shunt along the south coast of England before crossing the English Channel, especially if the weather is adverse.

Sibe   A Siberian SUBSPECIES of a SPECIES found in Europe, for example the SIBERIAN STONECHAT. It is a slang term used in RINGING and TWITCHING.

Siberian Stonechat   A Stonechat *Saxicola torquata* of one of the Asian

SUBSPECIES which have the SCIENTIFIC NAME *S.t. maura* or *S.t. stejnegeri*. (As well as the British breeding race *S.t. hibernans* there are several continental European subspecies). Birds showing the characters of these Siberian races (perhaps merely ABERRANT individuals of European subspecies) are rare visitors to the British Isles.

Sibling In human terms a brother or sister. Therefore, the chicks in a single brood are each other's siblings.

Sight record See HYPOTHETICAL SPECIES.

Significance See STATISTICALLY SIGNIFICANT.

Singing See SONG.

Single-brooded Laying a single CLUTCH during a BREEDING SEASON, although a REPLACEMENT may be laid if the first clutch is lost to a PREDATOR or is abandoned for some reason. Many SPECIES are normally single-brooded, but many others are 'double-brooded' and some, such as the Blackbird *Turdus merula* or the House Sparrow *Passer domesticus*, may be 'multi-brooded', laying three clutches in a single season.

Site of Special Scientific Interest A place which, although not given National NATURE RESERVE status, is, nevertheless, officially recognised by the NATURE CONSERVANCY COUNCIL as having importance for geology or BIOLOGY. Many places with SSSI status are important ornithologically.

Sites Register See REGISTER OF ORNITHOLOGICAL SITES.

Skein A small flock of flying geese (FAMILY Anatidae) usually referring to a ragged line or 'V' formation. Such a flock on the ground forms a 'gaggle'.

Skerry A very small marine island, sometimes just a rock. The use of this term is not precise, and a HOLM or STACK might be called a 'skerry'.

Skin A specimen which has been preserved by the methods used in TAXIDERMY. If a museum skin is not made up into a MOUNTED SPECIMEN for display, it will be stored for reference by ornithologists interested in such topics as MOULT or TAXONOMY.

Smoke bathing Deliberately visiting a source of smoke and allowing it to touch the feathers. Presumably smoke bathing discourages ECTOPARA-SITE infestation, and so is comparable to ANTING and DUSTING. It is well seen in Starlings *Sturnus vulgaris* on chimney tops.

Soaring See GLIDING.

Social display See LEK.

Social facilitation Learning through observation and imitation of others, also called 'local enhancement'. This phenomenon is best seen when a new habit is learned and spreads from one POPULATION to another, for example the opening of milk bottles on doorsteps by tits (FAMILY Paridae) in order to drink the cream, a habit first reported in Southampton in 1929 and now widespread.

Social nesting   See COLONY.

Society for the Promotion of Nature Conservation   An organisation founded in 1912 (as the 'Society for the Promotion of Nature Reserves') which now acts as a representative at national level for the members of the local NATURALISTS' TRUST movement. The SPNC publishes the quarterly bulletin 'CONSERVATION Review' and its headquarters are at Nettleham in Lincolnshire. Its junior section is called 'Watch'.

Soft parts   See BARE PARTS.

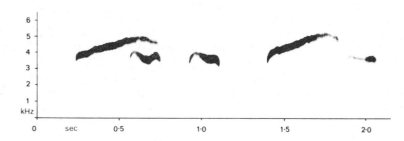

Sonagram   A visual representation of sound, in the form of a trace on a graph, in which the vertical axis shows frequency ('pitch'), being graduated in kiloHertz (kilocycles), and the horizontal axis shows duration (in seconds). The degree of blackness or greyness of the sound trace indicates loudness ('amplitude'). The word 'sonagram' is actually an abbreviation of 'sound-spectrogram', the machine used being a 'sonagraph' or 'sound-spectrograph'. A 'melogram' (produced by a 'melograph') is somewhat similar to a sonagram but analyses the frequency of the sound much more precisely and also shows its relative intensity in decibels (so that two graphs are produced). Sonagrams, and to a lesser extent melograms, are now widely used in the study of bird SONG and CALL notes.

Song   A more or less complex series of sounds produced by a (usually male) bird for the purposes of attracting a mate and/or defending a TERRITORY against others of its species. Bird song is not necessarily melodious, nor is it confined to the so-called 'songbirds' (OSCINES). Song is not always produced vocally, as a few species have INSTRUMENTAL SONG. All sounds made by birds which do not have the function of song are regarded as 'CALL notes'.

Songbird   See OSCINES.

Songbox   See SYRINX.

Song flight   Aerial production of SONG, as opposed to the use of a SONG POST. Song flights are typical of, but not confined to, those SPECIES which live in open types of HABITAT where elevated song posts may not be available, for example the Skylark *Alauda arvensis* and Meadow Pipit *Anthus pratensis*. There is some overlap between the concept of a song flight and that of a DISPLAY FLIGHT.

Song period   The part of the year during which the SONG of a particular SPECIES can be heard. Some birds, such as the Wren *Troglodytes troglodytes*, sing virtually all year round, but most have their song periods confined to part of the year. The Blackbird *Turdus merula*, for example, sings mainly between the end of February and early July.

Song post   A point from which SONG is delivered. As advertisement is one of the functions of song, many song posts are in conspicuous positions and often at some height, as, for example, those used by the thrushes of the GENUS *Turdus*. Birds which have skulking habits, however, may have song posts which are low down and concealed, as in the case of the Nightingale *Luscinia megarhynchos*.

Sound-spectrogram   See SONAGRAM.

SPATULATE BILL : SPOONBILL

Spatulate   Spoon- or shovel-shaped, a description applied to the bills of the Spoonbill *Platalea leucorodia* and the Shoveler *Anas clypeata*.

Speciation   The formation of a new SPECIES from an existing one by means of the process of EVOLUTION by NATURAL SELECTION.

Species   A POPULATION whose members breed among themselves but not (normally) with members of other similarly defined populations. The members of a particular species are said to be 'conspecific'. The species is the only division used in TAXONOMY which is actually defined in nature. Each species has been given a SCIENTIFIC NAME which consists of two parts, under the system of BINOMIAL NOMENCLATURE, the actual 'specific name' being the second of the two. Closely related species are placed in the same GENUS and most species are divided into SUBSPECIES.

Species diversity   The variety of SPECIES found in a particular HABITAT or locality. A MOOR, for example, has a lesser species diversity than BROAD-LEAVED woodland, while Great Britain has a higher species diversity than Ireland.

Species pair   Two very closely related and very similar SPECIES, for example the Crossbill *Loxia curvirostra* and the Scottish Crossbill *L. scotica*. In such cases there is often some doubt over the justification for regarding the two as separate species, and the Scottish Crossbill might be considered by some ornithologists to be simply a SUBSPECIES of the Crossbill. A group of very closely related species may be called a SUPERSPECIES.

Species-specific   Confined to one particular SPECIES.

Specific name   See BINOMIAL NOMENCLATURE and SPECIES.

SPECULUM : MALLARD

Speculum   A patch of colour on the wing of a duck (FAMILY Anatidae) contrasting with that of the rest of the wing. A speculum is a small WING PANEL, and may form an important identification aid.

Splitter   See LUMPER.

Sponsored birdwatch   A money-raising venture in which sponsors promise to pay a certain amount for each SPECIES which a birdwatcher records during a specified period. The ROYAL SOCIETY FOR THE PROTECTION OF BIRDS, for example, now organises such events.

Sport   A bird with ABERRANT characteristics, or a new VARIETY of CAGEBIRD. It is a term used in AVICULTURE.

Spottingscope   A PRISMATIC type of telescope, very compact because it does not use the DRAWTUBE method of focusing.

Spring   A small flock of Teal *Anas crecca* or similar small DABBLING DUCK, which have a rapid almost vertical take-off.

Spur   A bony outgrowth from the TARSUS covered with a horny sheath and having a sharp point, found, for example, in the male Pheasant *Phasianus colchicus*. Spurs are used in fighting and are capable of inflicting serious injury.

Squab   A young nestling pigeon or dove (FAMILY Columbidae), fed at least partly on PIGEON'S MILK. An older nestling is called a 'squeaker'.

Squeaker See SQUAB.

Squeaking A North American term for the practice of attempting to attract PASSERINE birds close to the observer by noisily sucking air through pursed lips or loudly kissing the back of the hand. It is also called 'pishing'.

Stack See SKERRY.

Standard deviation A STATISTICAL measure of the degree of variation ('spread') of a set of QUANTITATIVE data around its MEAN. It is important to know the standard deviation if the mean is to be of any real use, while the mean itself is subject to a STANDARD ERROR.

Standard error (of the mean) The difference between an observed MEAN (of a sample of QUANTITATIVE data) and the true mean. The latter could only be known if the data for the entire POPULATION could be collected instead of just a sample, which is usually impossible in ornithological studies, but STATISTICAL analysis of the data can suggest what the true mean might be, and can also provide 'confidence limits' which show, for example, that in 95% of cases such assessments of the mean will be correct.

Starring See CHIPPING.

Statistical In accordance with the theory and practice of statistics, which is concerned with the objective analysis of QUANTITATIVE data. Modern SCIENTIFIC study of birds increasingly involves the use of statistical methods to test whether apparent relationships between cause and effect really are STATISTICALLY SIGNIFICANT.

Statistically significant Not resulting from mere chance. If a relationship between one variable and another is subjected to STATISTICAL testing and is found to be real rather than simply coincidental, that relationship can be described as statistically significant. For example, in a case where egg laying date and BREEDING SUCCESS were apparently linked, if the data were tested for statistical significance the 'probability' of such a relationship occurring by chance would be indicated. Such probability is usually written in the form (for example) 'P < 0.01', meaning that in this case coincidence could be expected less than once in every hundred occurrences. Therefore tests of statistical significance greatly reduce the risk of incorrect interpretation of data, and so they are very useful in ornithological studies, where the data usually consist of very small samples of the total POPULATION.

Status The nature of a SPECIES' occurrence in a particular area. It denotes the frequency with which the bird is found, usually described vaguely by such terms as 'common' or 'scarce', and the seasonality of its use of the area, the bird being called a RESIDENT, SUMMER VISITOR, WINTER VISITOR or PASSAGE migrant, as appropriate.

Sternum The large bone to which the lower ends of the bird's ribs are attached, also called the 'breastbone'. It has a 'keel' or 'carina' along its lower edge to which the PECTORAL MUSCLES are anchored.

STIFFTAIL : RUDDY DUCK

Stifftail   A member of the TRIBE Oxyurini, being a small DIVING DUCK. No stifftails are native to the British Isles but one, the Ruddy Duck *Oxyura jamaicensis*, is well established as a FERAL bird.

Stoop   The spectacular, rapid dive of the hunting Peregrine *Falco peregrinus*, or similar RAPTOR.

Striated   Streaked.

Sub-adult   A bird which is still in the PLUMAGE of an IMMATURE but is involved in MOULT into ADULT plumage.

Subcutaneous fat   A layer of fat stored just underneath the skin to provide energy during MIGRATION, also called 'pre-migratory fat'. Its development causes a very noticeable increase in weight in a bird preparing for migration and it enables a migrant to travel long distances without having to stop for food, an invaluable aid in sea or desert crossings.

Subfamily   A division of a FAMILY, standing between the family and the TRIBE or GENUS in TAXONOMY. The SCIENTIFIC NAME of a subfamily ends in '-inae'. The WILDFOWL family (Anatidae) is divided into three subfamilies, of which two have representatives in the British Isles, namely the Anserinae (swans and geese) and the Anatinae (ducks).

Sub-moustachial stripe   See MOUSTACHIAL STRIPE.

Sub-order   A division of an ORDER, thus standing between the order and the FAMILY in TAXONOMY. The very large order Passeriformes, containing the PASSERINE birds, is divided into four sub-orders, of which only one, the OSCINES, has representatives in the British Isles.

Subsong   An abbreviated version of full SONG, delivered at a very low volume, usually with the bill closed.

Subspecies   A division of a SPECIES, referring to a POPULATION inhabiting a more or less definite geographical area and differing in some respect(s) from other populations of the species concerned. Subspecies are often called 'races'. The boundaries between subspecies, regarding both their geographical ranges and their physical characteristics, are usually blurred and the grading of one into another is called a 'cline'. The SCIENTIFIC NAME given to a subspecies involves the use of TRINO-MIAL NOMENCLATURE, although 'subspecific names' are not normally used nowadays unless they are relevant to the matter in hand. Few subspecies are sufficiently distinctive in appearance to have been given English names (and the use of these is discouraged), but the White Wagtail is an example, being the Continental race *Motacilla alba alba* of the Pied Wagtail, of which the British race is *M.a. yarrellii*.

Subspecific name   See SUBSPECIES and TRINOMIAL NOMENCLA-TURE.

Subterminal   See TERMINAL.

Suffused   Tinged or tinted. For example, the whitish parts of the PLUM-AGE of the Long-tailed Tit *Aegithalos caudatus* show a pink suffusion.

Summer migrant or **summer visitor**   A bird which uses a particular area for breeding only, not being present at all outside the BREEDING SEASON. There are many examples found in the British Isles, particularly small INSECTIVOROUS birds like warblers (FAMILY Sylviidae).

Sun compass   See ORIENTATION.

Superciliary stripe   A more or less prominent curving streak above a bird's eye, not to be confused with an EYE STRIPE. A good example is found in the Redwing *Turdus iliacus*.

Superspecies   A group of SPECIES which are so closely related that they could almost be regarded as belonging to a single species. For example, the Grey Heron *Ardea cinerea* could be said to form a superspecies with the Great Blue Heron *A. herodias* of North America.

Supplanting (attack)   A type of aggressive behaviour in which an individual flies at another which is perched, and when the latter flees the former simply lands on the spot just vacated. Supplanting attacks are seen during COURTSHIP and in the defence or acquisition of TERRITORY.

Supplementary plumage   See BASIC PLUMAGE.

Surface dipping   Immersing the head and neck in the water without UPENDING. This is a feeding movement which may be used in shallow water by an AQUATIC bird which is a SURFACE FEEDER.

Surface feeder   An AQUATIC bird which does not normally obtain its food by diving, for example a DABBLING DUCK.

Swamp   See MARSH.

Swan mark   See SWAN UPPING.

Swan song   The sound supposedly produced by a dying swan (GENUS *Cygnus*). The origin of the expression is uncertain but presumably it refers to the loud-voiced Whooper Swan *C. cygnus* or Bewick's Swan *C. columbianus*, rather than the Mute Swan *C. olor*. Possibly exhalation of air through the TRACHEA of a shot swan as it falls from the sky can activate the vocal cords and produce an unusual and melodious sound at times.

Swan-upping   The capture and MARKING of Mute Swans *Cygnus olor*. Traditionally swan-upping is carried out on the Thames by two of the City of London 'Livery Companies', namely the Vintners' and the Dyers' Companies, the birds having 'swan marks' cut into their bills.

Sympatric   Living in the same geographical area. The converse is 'allopatric'. For example, the Common Gull *Larus canus* and Herring Gull *L. argentatus* are sympatric, whereas the Common Gull and the Ring-billed Gull *L. delawarensis* of North America are allopatric.

Synchronous hatching   See ASYNCHRONOUS HATCHING.

SYNDACTYLE FOOT : KINGFISHER

Syndactyl(e)   Having the INNER TOE and middle toe fused for part of their length. This arrangement of the foot is found in the Kingfisher *Alcedo atthis*.

Synecology   See AUTECOLOGY.

Syrinx   The 'songbox' of a bird, situated at the point where the TRACHEA divides into two branches, each of which connects with a lung. The vibration of a MEMBRANE within the syrinx produces sounds. The adjective from 'syrinx' is 'syringeal'.

Systematic list   A list of bird SPECIES arranged in a 'systematic order' such as the WETMORE ORDER or the VOOUS ORDER. A typical BIRD REPORT contains a systematic list of birds recorded in the area and the period concerned, arranged by species.

Systematics   See TAXONOMY.

Taiga See BOREAL FOREST.

Tail coverts The small feathers covering the base of the tail. They are grouped as upper and lower tail coverts.

Tail streamer A slender elongated tail feather, as seen in the adult Swallow *Hirundo rustica*.

Talon A massive, sharp claw on the toe of a RAPTOR, used particularly for grasping, killing and tearing the victim.

Talon-grappling Interlocking of the feet by the members of a RAPTOR pair. This aerial DISPLAY is part of COURTSHIP and may involve one of the pair flying upside-down.

Tarsal joint See TARSUS.

Tarsus The part of a bird's leg between what appears to be a backward-facing 'knee' and what appears to be an 'ankle'. In fact the bird's true knee is always hidden under the feathers, and the apparent 'knee' (the 'tarsal joint') is the ankle and heel. Therefore the tarsus is really the part of the foot between the heel and the ball, so that a bird stands on its toes. The tarsus may also be called the 'shank', and its bone is called the 'tarsometatarsus'.

Taxidermy The art of preparing and preserving stuffed specimens of VERTEBRATE animals. The end product is a SKIN or a MOUNTED SPECIMEN. In 1976 the Guild of Taxidermists was formed to promote high standards of training and practice.

Taxon Any one of the divisions used in TAXONOMY. The main taxa are the PHYLUM, the CLASS, the ORDER, the FAMILY, the GENUS, the SPECIES and the SUBSPECIES.

Taxonomy The SCIENTIFIC classification of living things. Each taxonomic division (TAXON) is based on what is known or suspected of the EVOLUTION of the group concerned, mainly on the evidence of features of its ANATOMY, and each taxon is given a SCIENTIFIC NAME. Taxonomy is also called 'systematics' and, with regard to animals only, 'faunistics'.

Ten Rare Men See RARITIES COMMITTEE.

Terminal At the end. 'Subterminal' means 'almost at the end'. Terminal bands on the tail may form important identification features, as for example among IMMATURE gulls (FAMILY Laridae).

Terrestrial Living on land, as opposed to AQUATIC.

Territory A defended area. Territory size varies from pecking distance in the case of the Guillemot *Uria aalge* to several square kilometres in that of the Golden Eagle *Aquila chrysaetos*. 'Breeding territories' may or may not also be 'feeding territories'. Few types of birds maintain a territory outside the BREEDING SEASON, an example being the Robin *Erithacus rubecula*, although all birds, even when in flocks, usually keep their INDIVIDUAL DISTANCE. The functions of territories vary but obviously the breeding territory provides an area in which the pair can undertake COURTSHIP, COPULATION and nesting without interference from others of their SPECIES.

Tertial   See TERTIARY (FEATHER).

Tertiary (feather)   One of the inner flight feathers of a bird's wing, although not as important in flying as the PRIMARY or SECONDARY feathers. The tertiaries (also called 'tertials') are few in number and are embedded in the skin of a bird's 'upper ARM'. They are really the innermost secondaries. In a few cases the name 'tertiaries' may be applied to other feather groups, for example, where they are conspicuously long, the SCAPULAR feathers.

Tetrad   See GRID SQUARE.

Tetrices or **tetrix**   See WING COVERTS.

Theory   See HYPOTHESIS.

Thermoregulation   Maintenance of optimum body temperature, which in birds ranges from about 38 °C to about 43 °C according to SPECIES and its activity. As birds are 'warm-blooded' ('homoiothermal') they are able to keep themselves at an almost constant temperature independently of their ENVIRONMENT, although in cold conditions they fluff out their feathers to keep warm by trapping an insulating layer of air, and in hot weather they pant to allow excess body heat to escape via the RESPIRATORY SYSTEM (as birds are unable to sweat). Chicks lose heat rapidly because of their small size and need a certain amount of BROODING, which is essential for NIDICOLOUS nestlings until their feathers begin to grow as they cannot regulate their temperature before they have reached this stage, being 'cold-blooded' ('poikilothermal') until this time.

Thick-knee   An alternative name for the Stone Curlew *Burhinus oedicnemus*.

Thorax   The middle section of the body, containing the heart and lungs. The adjective from 'thorax' is 'thoracic'. The other body divisions are the head and the ABDOMEN.

Throat   The part of a bird's exterior immediately below the CHIN and above the BREAST. The adjective meaning 'of the throat' is 'gular'.

Tibiotarsus   See FIBULA.

Ticker or **tick-hunter**   See TWITCHING.

Tiercel   A male falcon (FAMILY Falconidae). The female is simply the 'falcon'.

Tippet A structure consisting of the hanging feathers which adorn the sides of the head of the Great Crested Grebe *Podiceps cristatus* in breeding PLUMAGE.

Tissue The material of which the body of an ORGANISM is composed. A particular tissue consists of a mass of similar cells which give it distinctive characteristics.

Tit bell A small more or less bell-shaped container, open at the bottom, in which fat or suet is lodged, the bell then being hung with its open end downwards so that only acrobatic birds like tits (FAMILY Paridae) can feed from it.

Titmouse The full version of the name 'tit', referring mainly to members of the FAMILY Paridae. 'Titmouse' is not normally used nowadays in the British Isles but is still current in North America.

Tomia The cutting edges of the bill.

Tomtit An alternative name for the Blue Tit *Parus caeruleus* or the Great Tit *P. major*.

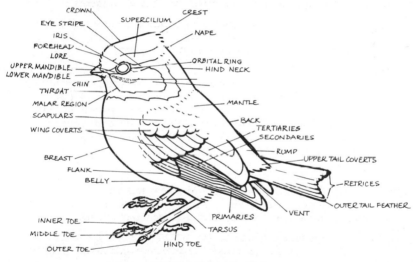

TOPOGRAPHY of a bird

Topography Description of the external features of a bird.

Top predator See FOOD CHAIN.

Torpid Having the bodily functions slowed. Torpidity is an energy-saving state which is not commonly found in birds in the British Isles, but is sometimes seen in nestlings of the Swift *Apus apus* when adverse weather prevents their parents providing sufficient insect food. In the absence of

THERMOREGULATION their body temperature drops at night, almost to that of the air, and so they become torpid.

TOTIPALMATE FOOT : GANNET

Totipalmate Having all the toes connected by webs instead of the more usual arrangement among AQUATIC birds where the HALLUX is free of webbing. In birds with totipalmate feet this 'hind' toe points forward like the others. The only ORDER of birds found in the British Isles and having this arrangement is the Pelecaniformes, containing the Gannet *Sula bassana*, Cormorant *Phalacrocorax carbo* and Shag *P. aristotelis*.

Toxic chemical A type of pesticide or industrial effluent which pollutes the ENVIRONMENT and is poisonous to life. The most persistently dangerous are those in the ORGANOCHLORINE group.

Transect A walk or drive across an area during which an observer records the numbers of birds found without deviating from a straight path. In a 'line transect' only those birds occurring on the track followed are recorded, whereas in a 'belt transect' the area within observational range on either side of the line is also covered. Where a transect crosses more than one type of HABITAT comparisons can be made regarding SPECIES DIVERSITY and POPULATION density.

Transient See PASSAGE.

Transplanting Moving captured birds to a new area and releasing them there. For example, Canada Geese *Branta canadensis* have been transplanted from districts where they have become too numerous.

Tree layer The highest vegetation zone, lying above the SHRUB LAYER, from about eight metres upwards. The tree tops themselves form the CANOPY.

Tribe A division used in TAXONOMY and standing between the SUB-FAMILY and the GENUS. The SCIENTIFIC NAME of a tribe ends in '-ini'. The wildfowl FAMILY (Anatidae) has ten tribes, representatives of six of which occur naturally in the British Isles, with FERAL members of two others also being present.

Trill A rapid succession of similar notes, as produced, for example, by the Little Grebe *Tachybaptus ruficollis*.

Trinomi(n)al nomenclature The system of applying a SCIENTIFIC NAME to a SUBSPECIES, involving the use of a third name added to those given to the GENUS and SPECIES under the rules of BINOMIAL NOMENCLATURE. The 'subspecific name', like the 'specific name', always has a small initial letter. One subspecies under each species has a subspecific name identical to the specific name, this being known as the 'nominate' subspecies. For example, in the case of the Blue Tit *Parus caeruleus* the nominate subspecies is the continental one, with the name *P.c. caeruleus*, while the one breeding in the British Isles is named *P.c. obscurus*.

Trip A group of Dotterels *Charadrius morinellus*.

Triumph ceremony A type of DISPLAY which follows a successful aggressive encounter, usually given by a pair of birds. It is well seen in the Whooper Swan *Cygnus cygnus* and the Bewick's Swan *C. columbianus*, and consists of raising the neck and wings and calling loudly.

Trophic level See FOOD CHAIN.

Trust for Nature Conservation See NATURALISTS' TRUST.

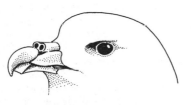

TUBE NOSE : FULMAR

Tubenose A member of the ORDER Procellariiformes, which contains the petrels and shearwaters. They have tubular nostrils lying along the top surface of the upper MANDIBLE, perhaps associated with the EXCRETION of excess salt or with a sense of smell which may be better developed than in most birds.

Tundra The area of open treeless country which encircles the Arctic Ocean, lying to the north of the belt of BOREAL FOREST. The vegetation consists mainly of mosses and lichens and much of the ground is boggy when it thaws in summer. It is an important breeding ground for many of the WILDFOWL and WADER flocks which visit the British Isles outside the BREEDING SEASON.

Turlough A shallow lake in a limestone area, usually containing water only during periods of wet weather and otherwise consisting of low-lying grassland. The term is used in western Ireland.

Turning down Releasing captive-bred birds into the wild. Certain SPE-

CIES of WILDFOWL and GALLINACEOUS birds are regularly turned down in order to improve the shooting.

Twilight factor A measure of the visual performance of binoculars or telescopes in poor light conditions. The factor is the square root of the product of the object lens (in mm) multiplied by the magnification, so that a 10 × 40 instrument has a twilight factor of $\sqrt{400} = 20$.

Twitching RARITY hunting, with perhaps an element of nervous excitement, particularly if there is the possibility of a LIFER. Twitchers are very mobile and may travel great distances to see rare birds, of which they hear through their efficient 'grapevine'. They may also be known as 'tickers', 'tick-hunters', 'listers' or 'birders', the latter two terms being used mainly in North America where 'birding', as opposed to 'birdwatching' is much more popular than in the British Isles.

Type The specimen used by the author who was the first to publish a proper description of the SPECIES concerned and to give it a SCIENTIFIC NAME. The type specimen may also be called a 'holotype', and the place where it was obtained is called the 'type locality'. The author's name, usually abbreviated, may be quoted after the scientific name of the species (similarly with a GENUS or a SUBSPECIES), for example *Parus caeruleus* Linn. (Blue Tit), the author in this case being LINNAEUS. If the species concerned, as a result of research in TAXONOMY, is now placed in a genus different from that originally proposed, the author's name is bracketed, for example, *Podiceps cristatus* (Linn.) (Great Crested Grebe), which Linnaeus placed in the genus *Colymbus*. If a newly described species is placed in a new genus, it becomes the 'type species' for that genus. As each FAMILY has a scientific name derived from that of one of the genera within it, the genus concerned is the 'type genus' for its family. For example, Fringillidae, the scientific name of the finch family, is formed from that of its type genus *Fringilla*.

Type genus See TYPE.

Type locality See TYPE.

Type species See TYPE.

Type specimen See TYPE.

Tystie An alternative name for the Black Guillemot *Cepphus grylle*, the term originating in Shetland but now widely used.

Ulna See RADIUS.

Ultimate factor One of the factors of the ENVIRONMENT which govern the year-cycles of birds in the ultimate analysis. For example, food supply is an ultimate factor controlling the timing of the BREEDING SEASON in any given SPECIES. The actual 'triggering' factor, however, may be one such as daylength or temperature, which has a direct effect on the birds' activities. These 'immediate' influences are called 'proximate factors'.

Underparts The CHIN, THROAT, BREAST, BELLY, FLANK and under TAIL COVERTS of a bird.

Understorey See SHRUB LAYER.

Under tail coverts See TAIL COVERTS.

Under wing coverts See WING COVERTS.

UP-ENDING : MALLARD

Upending Immersing the forepart of the body, head downwards, in the water, thus causing the hind part to stick up into the air. This position is maintained by paddling movements of the feet. Among AQUATIC birds upending is likely to be practised by a SURFACE FEEDER, in order to increase the depth to which it can reach.

Upperparts The MANTLE, BACK, RUMP and upper TAIL COVERTS of a bird. In descriptions of PLUMAGE the head, wings and tail are usually treated separately, and the tail coverts may be described along with the tail.

Upper tail coverts See TAIL COVERTS.

Upper wing coverts See WING COVERTS.

Uropygial gland See PREENING.

Uropygium See RUMP.

Vagrant A bird which wanders to a particular area if its ORIENTATION is at fault or adverse winds drive it off course but in normal circumstances would not be found there at all. Vagrants are also called 'accidentals' or 'casuals', and in the British Isles are usually defined as SPECIES which have been recorded less than 20 times. These islands are well placed to receive vagrants from various directions and a large proportion of the BRITISH LIST is made up of them.

Vane   See WEB.

Variety   A strain or breed of DOMESTIC livestock, the term not being used with reference to types of wild animals. Examples of varieties of domestic birds are Khaki Campbell and Indian Runner Ducks, both descended ultimately from the wild Mallard *Anas platyrhynchos*, despite their lack of resemblance to it and to each other.

Vascular system   The network of arteries, veins and lymph vessels in the body. The arterial system carries blood from the heart to the various parts of the body, the venous system returns the blood to the heart, and the lymphatic system carries the fluid which percolates from the blood into the body TISSUE.

Vent   See CLOACA.

Ventral   See DORSAL.

Vermiculated   Covered with a dense pattern of fine wavy lines. A good example of vermiculation is provided by the BACK of the Pochard *Aythya ferina*.

Vernacular name   See SCIENTIFIC NAME.

Vertebra   See VERTEBRATE.

Vertebral column   See VERTEBRATE.

Vertebrate   An animal with a backbone or 'vertebral column', which consists of a series of bony ring-like structures ('vertebrae') protecting the spinal cord. The vertebrates (fish, amphibians, reptiles, birds and mammals) form the 'sub-phylum' Vertebrata within the PHYLUM Chordata, each group of vertebrates forming a CLASS.

Vestigial   Present in a much reduced form, or only as a trace.

Vice-county   A division of a county for recording the DISTRIBUTION of plants (originally) and animals. There are 152 vice-counties in the British Isles (only 40 of them in Ireland) and, unlike the counties, each is of roughly comparable size. This system of mapping has now been replaced by the use of the GRID SQUARE as the basic unit, which allows much greater detail and avoids problems of changes in administrative boundaries and lack of exact comparability between units.

Vinaceous or **vinous**   Wine-coloured. The BREAST feathers of the drake Mallard *Anas platyrhynchos* can be so described.

Viscera   The soft internal parts (entrails). Visceral examination of birds found dead may reveal the effects of TOXIC CHEMICAL poisoning and other causes of death not obvious from external examination.

Visible migration The section of the stream of birds passing over an area on MIGRATION which can actually be seen from the ground. As most migration takes place at heights which are too great for the birds to be seen, visible migration may not be at all representative of the majority passing a particular MIGRATION WATCHPOINT.

Voous Order A sequence for listing birds devised by the Dutch ornithologist Professor K. H. Voous, first published in 1977. It is a modification of the older WETMORE ORDER and takes into account recent developments in TAXONOMY. The Voous Order is now used in most SCIENTIFIC work and has been adopted by the editors of the new HANDBOOK *The Birds of the Western Palearctic*. It is used wherever birds are listed in this dictionary, and the sequence for all the birds on the BRITISH LIST can be found in Appendix D.

Wader A member of the SUB-ORDER Limicolae in the ORDER Charadriiformes (waders, skuas, gulls, terns and auks). The majority of waders are placed either in the FAMILY Charadriidae (plovers) or in the family Scolopacidae (most other waders). The other wader families regularly represented in the British Isles are the Haematopodidae (oystercatchers), Recurvirostridae (avocets) and Burhinidae (stone curlews). The term 'wader' is not an accurate reflection of the habits of all the birds concerned and there are some 'wading birds' which lie outside its usual definition, such as the herons (family Ardeidae).

Wader Study Group An international organisation founded in 1970 with the aim of bringing together WADER enthusiasts and promoting the study of this group of birds. As well as acting as an information service it organises cooperative field studies and publishes a bulletin three times a year.

Wading bird See WADER.

Warble Any fairly musical sound made by a bird, the term not being precisely defined. The SONG of the Skylark *Alauda arvensis*, or the Blackbird *Turdus merula*, has a truly warbling quality, but some of the so-called 'warblers' (FAMILY Sylviidae) do not make warbling sounds.

Wash An area of low-lying land which is allowed to flood in order to release pressure caused by high river levels and so to prevent flooding elsewhere. The best example is found in the Fens, between Denver (Norfolk) and Earith (Cambridgeshire), and is known as the Ouse Washes. Over half of this area has NATURE RESERVE status. In summer it consists of grazing land, with breeding birds such as Black-tailed Godwit *Limosa limosa* and Snipe *Gallinago gallinago*, while the flooded washes in winter attract huge numbers of WILDFOWL including the largest flocks of Bewick's Swans *Cygnus columbianus* in the British Isles.

Watch   See SOCIETY FOR THE PROMOTION OF NATURE CONSERVA-
TION.

Watching back   Locating a nest by disturbing its owner, waiting for the
bird to return and noting exactly where it goes. This technique is useful
where nests are hidden in thick cover.

Waterfowl   See WILDFOWL.

Waterhen   An alternative name for the Moorhen *Gallinula chloropus*.

Water meadow   A riverside area of low-lying, regularly flooded grassland,
also called a 'flood meadow' and in some cases a WASH. Improved river
control is leading to the rapid disappearance of this kind of HABITAT,
which is important for birds such as the Lapwing *Vanellus vanellus* and
the Yellow Wagtail *Motacilla flava*.

Water Pipit   The SUBSPECIES of the Rock Pipit *Anthus spinoletta* breeding
in the mountains of southern Europe. It has the SCIENTIFIC NAME *A.s.
spinoletta*, the British breeding race being *A.s. petrosus*. The Water Pipit is
a very uncommon visitor to the British Isles.

Waterways Bird Survey   An annual census organised by the BRITISH
TRUST FOR ORNITHOLOGY which extends the techniques of the
COMMON BIRDS CENSUS to cover the birds of rivers and canals.

Wattle   A brightly coloured fleshy structure (also called a 'comb') on the
heads of certain SPECIES of birds, such as the Red Grouse *Lagopus
lagopus*. It is inflated when the bird is excited.

Weather movement   A shift in the winter quarters of a POPULATION of
birds in response to adverse weather, usually snow or hard frost. When
conditions improve the birds may or may not return to their original
wintering area. The movement can involve thousands of birds travelling
hundreds of kilometres, but it cannot be regarded as true MIGRATION
because of its irregularity and the lack of a definite return movement. The
Lapwing *Vanellus vanellus* often undertakes conspicuous weather movements, large numbers crossing the North Sea when icy conditions affect
the European continent, and moving on along with many British birds to
Ireland, western France and even Spain if Britain itself has a very cold
spell.

Web   The blade or vane of a feather, or the flange of skin joining the toes of
most AQUATIC types of birds.

Western Palearctic   See PALEARCTIC.

Wetland   Any area of fresh water or MARSH, including flowing water and
canals. A great deal of CONSERVATION effort has been focused on this

kind of HABITAT, whose continued existence is constantly threatened by drainage and reclamation.

Wetmore Order A sequence for listing bird SPECIES devised by the American ornithologist Alexander Wetmore round about 1930. It places related groups close to each other, starting with the most primitive and ending with the most advanced. The Wetmore Order is still the generally accepted sequence, although subsequent research in TAXONOMY has increased knowledge of the relationships between birds and therefore many modifications have been necessary. The most recent revised version is the VOOUS ORDER.

Whiffling Descending rapidly from a height once the decision to land has been made, involving fast side-slipping first one way and then the other. The term is usually applied to geese (FAMILY Anatidae), whose flocks whiffle spectacularly, especially when wishing to avoid a long, slow descent over an area where WILDFOWLING is practised.

Whisker See MOUSTACHIAL STRIPE.

White-spotted Bluethroat See RED-SPOTTED BLUETHROAT.

White Wagtail The SUBSPECIES of the Pied Wagtail *Motacilla alba* breeding on the European continent. It has the SCIENTIFIC NAME *M.a. alba*, the British breeding race being *M.a. yarrellii*. The White Wagtail is a PASSAGE migrant through the British Isles.

Wide-angle binoculars A pair of binoculars with a particularly wide FIELD OF VIEW, a desirable feature for the birdwatcher. Such an instrument may be designated by the letters 'W' or 'WA', for example '8 × 40W'. See diagram on page 51.

Wildfowl The members of the FAMILY Anatidae, which contains the swans, geese and ducks. The term 'waterfowl' may also be used to refer specifically to this family, particularly in North America, but this word can also have a wider meaning, covering birds other than wildfowl living on or beside water, such as the divers (family Gaviidae) and the grebes (family Podicipedidae).

Wildfowl count An annual series of counts of WILDFOWL organised by the WILDFOWL TRUST and covering major waters right across Britain. Observers count their local wildfowl on pre-arranged days once per month between September and March, when huge numbers of these birds from north and north-east Europe are present in the British Isles.

Wildfowlers' Association of Great Britain and Ireland An organisation founded in 1909 to represent the bird-shooters of the British Isles. It is active in the fields of CONSERVATION and research and cooperates closely with the WILDFOWL TRUST and similar bodies. WAGBI headquarters are at Rossett in Clwyd.

Wildfowling   The shooting of geese and duck (FAMILY Anatidae). The representative organisation is the WILDFOWLERS' ASSOCIATION OF GREAT BRITAIN AND IRELAND.

Wildfowl Refuge   A NATURE RESERVE established specifically to protect WILDFOWL, especially their winter flocks, as for example on the ESTUARY of the River Ribble.

Wildfowl Trust   An organisation founded by Sir Peter Scott in 1946 as the Severn Wildfowl Trust and concerned with the study and CONSERVATION of WILDFOWL throughout the world. The trust maintains collections of captive wildfowl and is a NATURE RESERVE owner. It publishes the annual journal 'Wildfowl' and a twice-yearly bulletin, 'Wildfowl World'. Its headquarters are at Slimbridge in Gloucestershire.

Wild swan   A name covering the Bewick's Swan *Cygnus columbianus* and the Whooper Swan *C. cygnus*, distinguishing these truly wild swans from the partly DOMESTICATED Mute Swan *C. olor*.

Willowchiff   A combination of the names Willow Warbler *Phylloscopus trochilus* and Chiffchaff *P. collybita*, used on those occasions when the observer is uncertain which of these two very similar SPECIES he has seen.

Window   A pale patch on the inner PRIMARY feathers of the wings of certain gulls (FAMILY Laridae), for example the JUVENILE Herring Gull *Larus argentatus*.

Wing bar   A line across the wing contrasting in colour with the rest of it. A long and fairly wide wing bar, such as that of the Black-tailed Godwit *Limosa limosa*, may be called a 'wing stripe'. Wing bars and stripes are important identification features in many SPECIES, for example in some types of WADER.

Wing clapping   Raising the wings and striking them together to produce a loud crack. This BEHAVIOUR is well seen in the Woodpigeon *Columba palumbus*, especially when it is startled or is on its DISPLAY FLIGHT.

Wing clip   See WING TAG.

Wing coverts   The small feathers which cover the bases of the PRIMARY, SECONDARY and TERTIARY feathers. They are also called 'tetrices' (singular 'tetrix') and are present on both the upper and lower surfaces of the wing, forming the 'upper wing coverts' and 'under wing coverts' (or 'wing lining') respectively. These feathers are arranged in four bands, namely (from the leading edge of the wing) the 'marginal', 'lesser', 'median' and 'greater' coverts. See diagram on page 7.

Winged   Hit by gunshot but not incapacitated. The term 'pricked' has a similar meaning. A more severely injured bird, unable to fly, is called a 'cripple'.

Wing formula   The arrangement of the tips of the PRIMARY feathers of a bird's wing, expressed as the amount by which each primary is shorter than the longest. Wing formulae can be useful in studies of MOULT and in the positive identification in the hand of very similar SPECIES.

Wing lining   See WING COVERTS.

Wing loading   The relationship between the surface area of the wings and the bird's weight. The higher the weight in proportion to the wing area, the higher is the wing loading. A bird with a low wing loading, such as a harrier (GENUS *Circus*), is more agile in the air and can fly more slowly than one with a high loading, such as a swan (genus *Cygnus*).

Wing panel   A more or less rectangular patch of colour on the wing, well seen in some of the ducks (FAMILY Anatidae), such as the Goldeneye *Bucephala clangula*. A small wing panel may be called a SPECULUM.

Wing stripe   See WING BAR.

Wing tag   A small clip fixed to the leading edge of a bird's wing so that it can be recognised as belonging to the marked POPULATION and its movements can be followed. A wing tag may also be called a 'patagial tag' because it is clipped to the PATAGIUM. The wing tag is a method of MARKING best used on relatively large birds.

Winnowing   Rapid wing beating through a very shallow arc in swift flight. It is characteristic of some falcons (FAMILY Falconidae), notably the Hobby *Falco subbuteo* and the Peregrine *F. peregrinus*, which alternate winnowing with GLIDING on outstretched wings.

Winter distribution or **winter range**   See DISTRIBUTION.

Winter visitor   A bird which visits a particular area only for the winter and does not breed there, although others of its SPECIES may do so. As the British Isles have a milder winter climate than places to the north and east, they play host to many winter visitors from those areas. Some of these birds belong to species which breed in the British Isles, such as the Lapwing *Vanellus vanellus* and the Starling *Sturnus vulgaris*, while others are normally known only as winter visitors, such as the Barnacle Goose *Branta leucopsis* and the Brambling *Fringilla montifringilla*.

Wishbone   See PECTORAL GIRDLE.

Wisp   A small flock of Snipe *Gallinago gallinago*.

Wood warbler   See NEW WORLD WARBLER.

World Wildlife Fund   An organisation founded in 1961 to raise money for CONSERVATION of animals anywhere in the world. The world headquarters are at Morges in Switzerland and the British branch (the 'British National Appeal') is based in London.

Wreck   An incident involving a large number of SEABIRD deaths over a short period of time. Storms at sea can be responsible for wrecks and if they include strong onshore winds many seabirds can be stranded far inland. Mass deaths can also result from OILING or poisoning by natural or man-made substances.

Xanthism or **xanthochroism**   An ABERRANT condition involving the presence of an excessive amount of yellow pigment in the feathers.

Yaffle   An alternative name for the Green Woodpecker *Picus viridis*, referring to its laughing CALL.

Year-cycle   The complete sequence of a bird's activities through the year. For bird study, a year which begins after the MOULT in late summer is perhaps more meaningful than the calendar year.

Year list   A list of the birds seen during a particular year. Many birdwatchers keep such lists, with no serious purpose.

Yellow Bunting   An alternative name for the Yellowhammer *Emberiza citrinella*.

Young Ornithologists' Club   The junior wing of the ROYAL SOCIETY FOR THE PROTECTION OF BIRDS, founded in 1965 as a successor to the Junior Bird Recorders' Club. It caters for young people up to the age of 18 and is much involved in education. It publishes the quarterly magazine 'Bird Life' and it is based at the RSPB headquarters at Sandy in Bedfordshire.

Zoogeographical Region   One of the six geographical divisions of the world devised for the study of the DISTRIBUTION of land animals, also called 'faunal regions'. They consist of the PALEARCTIC, the Nearctic (North America), the Neotropical (South America), the Afrotropical (formerly 'Ethiopian') (Africa south of the Sahara), the Oriental (Asia south of the Himalayas) and the Australasian (Australia, New Zealand and nearby islands). Antarctica forms an additional region.

Zoological Society of London   An organisation founded in 1826 for the scientific study of animals anywhere in the world. Its headquarters are at Regent's Park in London.

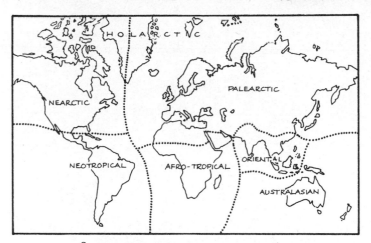

See ZOOGEOGRAPHICAL REGION opposite

Zoology The SCIENTIFIC study of animals, of which the academic side of ornithology forms a part. It is a branch of BIOLOGY. University departments of zoology which have a close connection with ornithology are those at Oxford (through the EDWARD GREY INSTITUTE OF FIELD ORNITHOLOGY), Durham and Aberdeen.

Zoom The facility of changing magnification quickly and smoothly without the necessity of taking the eyes off the object being viewed. Zoom telescopes are frequently used by birdwatchers but the zoom facility is not thought necessary for binoculars, and is seldom found.

Zoonosis A disease capable of transmission from birds to humans. A good example is PSITTACOSIS.

Zugunruhe See MIGRATORY RESTLESSNESS.

ZYGODACTYLE FOOT : WOODPECKER

Zygodactyl(e) Having two toes facing forwards and two backwards, instead of the more usual arrangement where three face forwards and one backwards. Zygodactyle feet are found in the woodpeckers (FAMILY Picidae) as an aid to climbing and perching vertically on the trunks of trees.

Abbreviations

ad	adult
BANC	British Association of Nature Conservationists
BB	'British Birds' (journal)
BLOWS	British Library of Wildlife Sounds
BNA	British National Appeal (World Wildlife Fund); British Naturalists' Association
BO	Bird Observatory
BOC	Bird Observatories Council; British Ornithologists' Club
BOU	British Ornithologists' Union
BRC	Biological Records Centre
BTCV	British Trust for Conservation Volunteers
BTO	British Trust for Ornithology
BWP	(The) Birds of the Western Palearctic (handbook)
c/	clutch of (followed by number of eggs)
CBC	Common Birds Census
CfN	Council for Nature (now defunct)
CoEnCo	Council for Environmental Conservation
EGI	Edward Grey Institute (of Field Ornithology)
EOAC	European Ornithological Atlas Committee
f	female
FC	Field Club
FLS	Fellow of the Linnean Society (of London)
FPS	Fauna Preservation Society
FSC	Field Studies Council
FWAG	Farming and Wildlife Advisory Group
FZS	Fellow of the Zoological Society (of London)
ICBP	International Council for Bird Preservation
imm	immature
IOC	International Ornithological Committee/Congress
IRP	Irish Records Panel

ITE	Institute of Terrestrial Ecology
IUCN	International Union for the Conservation of Nature (and Natural Resources)
IWC	Irish Wildbird Conservancy
IWRB	International Waterfowl Research Bureau
juv	juvenile
L or Linn	Linnaeus
LNR	Local Nature Reserve
m	male
MBOU	Member of the British Ornithologists' Union
NCC	Nature Conservancy Council
NCT	Nature Conservation Trust
NERC	Natural Environment Research Council
NHS	Natural History Society
NNR	National Nature Reserve
NR	Nature Reserve
NT	National Trust; Naturalists' Trust
P	probability (statistical)
PCB	polychlorinated biphenyl (toxic chemical)
pers. comm.	personal communication
RBC	Rare Birds Committee
RC	Records Committee; Rarities Committee
RG	Ringing Group
RSPB	Royal Society for the Protection of Birds
SFSA	Scottish Field Studies Association
SOC	Scottish Ornithologists' Club
sp.	species (singular)
SPNC	Society for the Promotion of Nature Conservation
spp.	species (plural)
ssp.	subspecies
SSSI	Site of Special Scientific Interest
TNC	Trust for Nature Conservation
WAGBI	Wildfowlers' Association of Great Britain and Ireland
WR	Wildfowl Refuge
WT	Wildfowl Trust; Wildlife Trust
WWF	World Wildlife Fund
YOC	Young Ornithologists' Club
♂	male

♂♂	males
♀	female
♀♀	females
<	less than
>	more than

North American Names

Bird species which are found both in Europe and in North America may be called by different English names in the two continents. For those species in which such differences exist, the names which are normally used in North American bird publications are listed below with their British equivalents and scientific names. If a species which occurs on both sides of the Atlantic does not appear on the list, as for example Sanderling *Calidris alba* or Raven *Corvus corax*, it can be assumed that it usually has the same English name in the Old and New Worlds. It should also be noted that in some cases the British version may be used even if a North American alternative exists, many Hudsonian Curlews, for example, being called Whimbrels.

North American name	*British name*	*Scientific name*
Auk, Razor-billed	Razorbill	*Alca torda*
Baldpate	American Wigeon	*Anas americana*
Brant	Brent Goose	*Branta bernicla*
Creeper, Brown	Treecreeper	*Certhia familiaris*
Crossbill, Red	Crossbill	*Loxia curvirostra*
Crossbill, White-winged	Two-barred Crossbill	*L. leucoptera*
Curlew, Hudsonian	Whimbrel	*Numenius phaeopus*
Dovekie	Little Auk	*Alle alle*
Eagle, Gray Sea	White-tailed Eagle	*Haliaeetus albicilla*
Egret, American/ Common	Great White Egret	*Egretta alba*
Gallinule, Common/ Florida	Moorhen	*Gallinula chloropus*
Grebe, Eared	Black-necked Grebe	*Podiceps nigricollis*
Grebe, Holboell's	Red-necked Grebe	*P. grisegena*
Grebe, Horned	Slavonian Grebe	*P. auritus*
Gull, Mew/Short-billed	Common Gull	*Larus canus*
Hawk, Duck	Peregrine	*Falco peregrinus*
Hawk, Fish	Osprey	*Pandion haliaetus*

North American name	British name	Scientific name
Hawk, Marsh	Hen Harrier	*Circus cyaneus*
Hawk, Pigeon	Merlin	*Falco columbarius*
Hawk, Rough-legged	Rough-legged Buzzard	*Buteo lagopus*
Heron, Black-crowned Night	Night Heron	*Nycticorax nycticorax*
Jaeger, Long-tailed	Long-tailed Skua	*Stercorarius longicaudus*
Jaeger, Parasitic	Arctic Skua	*S. parasiticus*
Jaeger, Pomarine	Pomarine Skua	*S. pomarinus*
Kittiwake, Black-legged	Kittiwake	*Rissa tridactyla*
Knot, Red	Knot	*Calidris canutus*
Lark, Horned	Shore Lark	*Eremophila alpestris*
Longspur, Lapland	Lapland Bunting	*Calcarius lapponicus*
Loon, Common	Great Northern Diver	*Gavia immer*
Loon, Pacific	Black-throated Diver	*G. arctica*
Loon, Red-throated	Red-throated Diver	*G. stellata*
Loon, Yellow-billed	White-billed Diver	*G. adamsii*
Magpie, Black-billed	Magpie	*Pica pica*
Merganser, American/ Common	Goosander	*Mergus merganser*
Murre, Brünnich's/ Thick-billed	Brünnich's Guillemot	*Uria lomvia*
Murre, Common	Guillemot	*U. aalge*
Oldsquaw	Long-tailed Duck	*Clangula hyemalis*
Owl, Boreal/Richardson's	Tengmalm's Owl	*Aegolius funereus*
Partridge, Hungarian	Grey Partridge	*Perdix perdix*
Phalarope, Northern	Red-necked Phalarope	*Phalaropus lobatus*
Phalarope, Red	Grey Phalarope	*P. fulicarius*
Pheasant, Ring-necked	Pheasant	*Phasianus colchicus*
Pipit, American	Rock Pipit	*Anthus spinoletta*
Plover, Black-bellied	Grey Plover	*Pluvialis squatarola*
Plover, Semipalmated	Ringed Plover	*Charadrius hiaticula*
Plover, Snowy	Kentish Plover	*C. alexandrinus*
Plover, Upland	Upland Sandpiper	*Bartramia longicauda*
Ptarmigan, Rock	Ptarmigan	*Lagopus mutus*
Ptarmigan, Willow	Red/Willow Grouse	*L. lagopus*
Puffin, Atlantic/Common	Puffin	*Fratercula arctica*

North American name	British name	Scientific name
Redpoll, Hoary	Arctic Redpoll	*Carduelis hornemanni*
Robin	American Robin	*Turdus migratorius*
Sandpiper, Red-backed	Dunlin	*Calidris alpina*
Scoter, American	Common Scoter	*Melanitta nigra*
Scoter, White-winged	Velvet Scoter	*M. fusca*
Shrike, Northern	Great Grey Shrike	*Lanius excubitor*
Skua	Great Skua	*Stercorarius skua*
Snipe, Wilson's	Snipe	*Gallinago gallinago*
Sparrow, English	House Sparrow	*Passer domesticus*
Swallow, Bank	Sand Martin	*Riparia riparia*
Swallow, Barn	Swallow	*Hirundo rustica*
Tern, Cabot's	Sandwich Tern	*Sterna sandvicensis*
Tern, Least	Little Tern	*S. albifrons*
Turnstone, Ruddy	Turnstone	*Arenaria interpres*
Waxwing, Bohemian	Waxwing	*Bombycilla garrulus*
Wren, Winter	Wren	*Troglodytes troglodytes*

Birdwatcher's Code of Conduct

The code of practice for birdwatchers, summarised below, resulted from consultation between the British Ornithologists' Union, the British Trust for Ornithology, the Royal Society for the Protection of Birds, the Scottish Ornithologists' Club, the Wildfowl Trust and the editors of the journal 'British Birds'. The code, the ten basic points of which are given below, was first published in the RSPB magazine 'Birds' in summer 1980 (Vol. 8, No. 2, p. 67).

1 The welfare of birds must come first.
2 Habitat must be protected.
3 Keep disturbance to birds and their habitat to a minimum.
4 When you find a rare bird think carefully about whom you should tell.
5 Do not harass rare migrants.
6 Abide by the Bird Protection Acts at all times.
7 Respect the rights of landowners.
8 Respect the rights of other people in the countryside.
9 Make your records available to the local bird recorder.
10 Behave abroad as you would when birdwatching at home.

The British and Irish List
(Voous Order)

The species of birds on the British and Irish List at 1st January 1980 are named below, grouped into their orders and families. They are arranged in the 'Voous Order', the sequence devised by K.H. Voous (*List of Recent Holarctic Bird Species*, British Ornithologists' Union, 1977) and which is now generally accepted as standard by ornithologists. The scientific names also follow Professor Voous, and the English names are those in general currency in British and Irish ornithology. The sequence and nomenclature of this appendix are used throughout the dictionary.

The letters (A, B, C and D) beside the names of species refer to the four categories of status in Britain and Ireland used by the British Ornithologists' Union and the Irish Wildbird Conservancy, the joint keepers of the British and Irish List. These categories are defined as follows (*The Status of Birds in Britain and Ireland*, British Ornithologists' Union, 1971):

A   Species which have been recorded in an apparently wild state in Britain or Ireland at least once within the last 50 years.

B   Species which have been recorded in an apparently wild state in Britain or Ireland at least once, but not within the last 50 years.

C   Species which, although originally introduced by man, have now established a regular feral breeding stock which apparently maintains itself without necessary recourse to further introduction.

D   Species which have been recorded within the last 50 years and would otherwise appear in Category A except that (1) there is a reasonable doubt that they have ever occurred in a wild state, or (2) they have certainly arrived with ship-assistance, or (3) they have only ever been found dead on the tide-line; also species which would otherwise appear in Category C, except that their feral breeding populations may or may not be self-supporting.

Order GAVIIFORMES
Family GAVIIDAE (divers)
Red-throated Diver *Gavia stellata* A
Black-throated Diver *G. arctica* A
Great Northern Diver *G. immer* A
White-billed Diver *G. adamsii* A

Order PODICIPEDIFORMES
Family PODICIPEDIDAE (grebes)
Pied-billed Grebe *Podilymbus podiceps* A
Little Grebe *Tachybaptus ruficollis* A
Great Crested Grebe *Podiceps cristatus* A
Red-necked Grebe *P. grisegena* A
Slavonian Grebe *P. auritus* A
Black-necked Grebe *P. nigricollis* A

Order PROCELLARIIFORMES
Family DIOMEDEIDAE (albatrosses)
Black-browed Albatross *Diomedea melanophris* A
Family PROCELLARIIDAE (petrels and shearwaters)
Fulmar *Fulmarus glacialis* A
Capped Petrel *Pterodroma hasitata* B
Bulwer's Petrel *Bulweria bulwerii* A
Cory's Shearwater *Calonectris diomedea* A
Great Shearwater *Puffinus gravis* A
Sooty Shearwater *P. griseus* A
Manx Shearwater *P. puffinus* A
Little Shearwater *P. assimilis* A
Family HYDROBATIDAE (storm petrels)
Wilson's Petrel *Oceanites oceanicus* A
White-faced Petrel *Pelagodroma marina* B
Storm Petrel *Hydrobates pelagicus* A
Leach's Petrel *Oceanodroma leucorhoa* A
Madeiran Petrel *O. castro* A

Order PELECANIFORMES
Family SULIDAE (gannets)
Gannet *Sula bassana* A
Family PHALACROCORACIDAE (cormorants)
Cormorant *Phalacrocorax carbo* A
Shag *P. aristotelis* A
Family PELECANIDAE (pelicans)
White Pelican *Pelecanus onocrotalus* D
Family FREGATIDAE (frigatebirds)
Magnificent Frigatebird *Fregata magnificens* A

Order CICONIIFORMES
  Family ARDEIDAE (herons)

Bittern *Botaurus stellaris*	A
American Bittern *B. lentiginosus*	A
Little Bittern *Ixobrychus minutus*	A
Night Heron *Nycticorax nycticorax*	A
Green Heron *Butorides striatus*	B
Squacco Heron *Ardeola ralloides*	A
Cattle Egret *Bubulcus ibis*	A
Little Egret *Egretta garzetta*	A
Great White Egret *E. alba*	A
Grey Heron *Ardea cinerea*	A
Purple Heron *A. purpurea*	A

  Family CICONIIDAE (storks)

Black Stork *Ciconia nigra*	A
White Stork *C. ciconia*	A

  Family THRESKIORNITHIDAE (ibises)

Glossy Ibis *Plegadis falcinellus*	A
Spoonbill *Platalea leucorodia*	A

Order PHOENICOPTERIFORMES
  Family PHOENICOPTERIDAE (flamingos)

Greater Flamingo *Phoenicopterus ruber*	D

Order ANSERIFORMES
  Family ANATIDAE (wildfowl)

Mute Swan *Cygnus olor*	A
Bewick's Swan *C. columbianus*	A
Whooper Swan *C. cygnus*	A
Bean Goose *Anser fabalis*	A
Pink-footed Goose *A. brachyrhynchos*	A
White-fronted Goose *A. albifrons*	A
Lesser White-fronted Goose *A. erythropus*	A
Greylag Goose *A. anser*	A
Snow Goose *A. caerulescens*	A
Canada Goose *Branta canadensis*	A
Barnacle Goose *B. leucopsis*	A
Brent Goose *B. bernicla*	A
Red-breasted Goose *B. ruficollis*	A
Egyptian Goose *Alopochen aegyptiacus*	C
Ruddy Shelduck *Tadorna ferruginea*	A
Shelduck *T. tadorna*	A
Wood Duck *Aix sponsa*	D
Mandarin *A. galericulata*	C
Wigeon *Anas penelope*	A
American Wigeon *A. americana*	A
Gadwall *A. strepera*	A

Order ANSERIFORMES (*cont.*)

Baikal Teal *A. formosa*	D
Teal *A. crecca*	A
Mallard *A. platyrhynchos*	A
Black Duck *A. rubripes*	A
Pintail *A. acuta*	A
Garganey *A. querquedula*	A
Blue-winged Teal *A. discors*	A
Shoveler *A. clypeata*	A
Red-crested Pochard *Netta rufina*	A
Pochard *Aythya ferina*	A
Ring-necked Duck *A. collaris*	A
Ferruginous Duck *A. nyroca*	A
Tufted Duck *A. fuligula*	A
Scaup *A. marila*	A
Eider *Somateria mollissima*	A
King Eider *S. spectabilis*	A
Steller's Eider *Polysticta stelleri*	A
Harlequin Duck *Histrionicus histrionicus*	A
Long-tailed Duck *Clangula hyemalis*	A
Common Scoter *Melanitta nigra*	A
Surf Scoter *M. perspicillata*	A
Velvet Scoter *M. fusca*	A
Bufflehead *Bucephala albeola*	A
Goldeneye *B. clangula*	A
Hooded Merganser *Mergus cucullatus*	A
Smew *M. albellus*	A
Red-breasted Merganser *M. serrator*	A
Goosander *M. merganser*	A
Ruddy Duck *Oxyura jamaicensis*	C

Order ACCIPITRIFORMES

Family ACCIPITRIDAE (hawks, eagles and vultures)

Honey Buzzard *Pernis apivorus*	A
Black Kite *Milvus migrans*	A
Red Kite *M. milvus*	A
White-tailed Eagle *Haliaeetus albicilla*	A
Egyptian Vulture *Neophron percnopterus*	B
Griffon Vulture *Gyps fulvus*	B
Marsh Harrier *Circus aeruginosus*	A
Hen Harrier *C. cyaneus*	A
Pallid Harrier *C. macrourus*	A
Montagu's Harrier *C. pygargus*	A
Goshawk *Accipiter gentilis*	A
Sparrowhawk *A. nisus*	A
Buzzard *Buteo buteo*	A
Rough-legged Buzzard *B. lagopus*	A

Spotted Eagle *Aquila clanga*   B
Golden Eagle *A. chrysaetos*   A
Family PANDIONIDAE (osprey)
  Osprey *Pandion haliaetus*   A

Order FALCONIFORMES
Family FALCONIDAE (falcons)
  Lesser Kestrel *Falco naumanni*   A
  Kestrel *F. tinnunculus*   A
  American Kestrel *F. sparverius*   A
  Red-footed Falcon *F. vespertinus*   A
  Merlin *F. columbarius*   A
  Hobby *F. subbuteo*   A
  Eleonora's Falcon *F. eleonorae*   A
  Gyrfalcon *F. rusticolus*   A
  Peregrine *F. peregrinus*   A

Order GALLIFORMES
Family TETRAONIDAE (grouse)
  Red/Willow Grouse *Lagopus lagopus*   A
  Ptarmigan *L. mutus*   A
  Black Grouse *Tetrao tetrix*   A
  Capercaillie *T. urogallus*   C
Family PHASIANIDAE (partridges and pheasants)
  Bobwhite *Colinus virginianus*   D
  Red-legged Partridge *Alectoris rufa*   C
  Grey Partridge *Perdix perdix*   A
  Quail *Coturnix coturnix*   A
  Reeves's Pheasant *Syrmaticus reevesii*   D
  Pheasant *Phasianus colchicus*   C
  Golden Pheasant *Chrysolophus pictus*   C
  Lady Amherst's Pheasant *C. amherstiae*   C

Order GRUIFORMES
Family RALLIDAE (rails)
  Water Rail *Rallus aquaticus*   A
  Spotted Crake *Porzana porzana*   A
  Sora Rail *P. carolina*   A
  Little Crake *P. parva*   A
  Baillon's Crake *P. pusilla*   A
  Corncrake *Crex crex*   A
  Moorhen *Gallinula chloropus*   A
  Allen's Gallinule *Porphyrula alleni*   B
  American Purple Gallinule *P. martinica*   A
  Coot *Fulica atra*   A
Family GRUIDAE (cranes)
  Crane *Grus grus*   A

Order GRUIFORMES (*cont.*)
    Sandhill Crane *G. canadensis*   B
    Family OTIDIDAE (bustards)
        Little Bustard *Tetrax tetrax*   A
        Houbara Bustard *Chlamydotis undulata*   A
        Great Bustard *Otis tarda*   A

Order CHARADRIIFORMES
    Family HAEMATOPODIDAE (oystercatchers)
        Oystercatcher *Haematopus ostralegus*   A
    Family RECURVIROSTRIDAE (stilts and avocets)
        Black-winged Stilt *Himantopus himantopus*   A
        Avocet *Recurvirostra avosetta*   A
    Family BURHINIDAE (stone curlews)
        Stone Curlew *Burhinus oedicnemus*   A
    Family GLAREOLIDAE (coursers and pratincoles)
        Cream-coloured Courser *Cursorius cursor*   A
        Collared Pratincole *Glareola pratincola*   A
        Black-winged Pratincole *G. nordmanni*   A
    Family CHARADRIIDAE (plovers)
        Little Ringed Plover *Charadrius dubius*   A
        Ringed Plover *C. hiaticula*   A
        Semipalmated Plover *C. semipalmatus*   A
        Killdeer *C. vociferus*   A
        Kentish Plover *C. alexandrinus*   A
        Greater Sand Plover *C. leschenaultii*   A
        Caspian Plover *C. asiaticus*   B
        Dotterel *C. morinellus*   A
        Lesser Golden Plover *Pluvialis dominica*   A
        Golden Plover *P. apricaria*   A
        Grey Plover *P. squatarola*   A
        Sociable Plover *Chettusia gregaria*   A
        White-tailed Plover *C. leucura*   A
        Lapwing *Vanellus vanellus*   A
    Family SCOLOPACIDAE (sandpipers)
        Knot *Calidris canutus*   A
        Sanderling *C. alba*   A
        Semipalmated Sandpiper *C. pusilla*   A
        Western Sandpiper *C. mauri*   A
        Little Stint *C. minuta*   A
        Temminck's Stint *C. temminckii*   A
        Least Sandpiper *C. minutilla*   A
        White-rumped Sandpiper *C. fuscicollis*   A
        Baird's Sandpiper *C. bairdii*   A
        Pectoral Sandpiper *C. melanotos*   A
        Sharp-tailed Sandpiper *C. acuminata*   A
        Curlew Sandpiper *C. ferruginea*   A

Purple Sandpiper *C. maritima*   A

Dunlin *C. alpina*   A

Broad-billed Sandpiper *Limicola falcinellus*   A

Stilt Sandpiper *Micropalama himantopus*   A

Buff-breasted Sandpiper *Tryngites subruficollis*   A

Ruff *Philomachus pugnax*   A

Jack Snipe *Lymnocryptes minimus*   A

Snipe *Gallinago gallinago*   A

Great Snipe *G. media*   A

Short-billed Dowitcher *Limnodromus griseus*   A

Long-billed Dowitcher *L. scolopaceus*   A

Woodcock *Scolopax rusticola*   A

Black-tailed Godwit *Limosa limosa*   A

Bar-tailed Godwit *L. lapponica*   A

Eskimo Curlew *Numenius borealis*   B

Whimbrel *N. phaeopus*   A

Curlew *N. arquata*   A

Upland Sandpiper *Bartramia longicauda*   A

Spotted Redshank *Tringa erythropus*   A

Redshank *T. totanus*   A

Marsh Sandpiper *T. stagnatilis*   A

Greenshank *T. nebularia*   A

Greater Yellowlegs *T. melanoleuca*   A

Lesser Yellowlegs *T. flavipes*   A

Solitary Sandpiper *T. solitaria*   A

Green Sandpiper *T. ochropus*   A

Wood Sandpiper *T. glareola*   A

Terek Sandpiper *Xenus cinereus*   A

Common Sandpiper *Actitis hypoleucos*   A

Spotted Sandpiper *A. macularia*   A

Turnstone *Arenaria interpres*   A

Wilson's Phalarope *Phalaropus tricolor*   A

Red-necked Phalarope *P. lobatus*   A

Grey Phalarope *P. fulicarius*   A

Family STERCORARIIDAE (skuas)

    Pomarine Skua *Stercorarius pomarinus*   A

    Arctic Skua *S. parasiticus*   A

    Long-tailed Skua *S. longicaudus*   A

    Great Skua *S. skua*   A

Family LARIDAE (gulls)

    Great Black-headed Gull *Larus ichthyaetus*   A

    Mediterranean Gull *L. melanocephalus*   A

    Laughing Gull *L. atricilla*   A

    Franklin's Gull *L. pipixcan*   A

    Little Gull *L. minutus*   A

    Sabine's Gull *L. sabini*   A

    Bonaparte's Gull *L. philadelphia*   A

Order CHARADRIIFORMES (*cont.*)
  Black-headed Gull *L. ridibundus*　　A
  Slender-billed Gull *L. genei*　　A
  Ring-billed Gull *L. delawarensis*　　A
  Common Gull *L. canus*　　A
  Lesser Black-backed Gull *L. fuscus*　　A
  Herring Gull *L. argentatus*　　A
  Iceland Gull *L. glaucoides*　　A
  Glaucous Gull *L. hyperboreus*　　A
  Great Black-backed Gull *L. marinus*　　A
  Ross's Gull *Rhodostethia rosea*　　A
  Kittiwake *Rissa tridactyla*　　A
  Ivory Gull *Pagophila eburnea*　　A
  Family STERNIDAE (terns)
    Gull-billed Tern *Gelochelidon nilotica*　　A
    Caspian Tern *Sterna caspia*　　A
    Royal Tern *S. maxima*　　A
    Sandwich Tern *S. sandvicensis*　　A
    Roseate Tern *S. dougallii*　　A
    Common Tern *S. hirundo*　　A
    Arctic Tern *S. paradisaea*　　A
    Bridled Tern *S. anaethetus*　　A
    Sooty Tern *S. fuscata*　　A
    Little Tern *S. albifrons*　　A
    Whiskered Tern *Chlidonias hybridus*　　A
    Black Tern *C. niger*　　A
    White-winged Black Tern *C. leucopterus*　　A
  Family ALCIDAE (auks)
    Guillemot *Uria aalge*　　A
    Brünnich's Guillemot *U. lomvia*　　A
    Razorbill *Alca torda*　　A
    Great Auk *Pinguinus impennis*　　B
    Black Guillemot *Cepphus grylle*　　A
    Little Auk *Alle alle*　　A
    Puffin *Fratercula arctica*　　A

Order PTEROCLIDIFORMES
  Family PTEROCLIDIDAE (sandgrouse)
    Pallas's Sandgrouse *Syrrhaptes paradoxus*　　A

Order COLUMBIFORMES
  Family COLUMBIDAE (doves)
    Rock Dove *Columba livia*　　A
    Stock Dove *C. oenas*　　A
    Woodpigeon *C. palumbus*　　A
    Collared Dove *Streptopelia decaocto*　　A
    Turtle Dove *S. turtur*　　A
    Rufous Turtle Dove *S. orientalis*　　A

Order PSITTACIFORMES
Family PSITTACIDAE (parrots)
Ring-necked Parakeet *Psittacula krameri*   D

Order CUCULIFORMES
Family CUCULIDAE (cuckoos)
Great Spotted Cuckoo *Clamator glandarius*   A
Cuckoo *Cuculus canorus*   A
Black-billed Cuckoo *Coccyzus erythrophthalmus*   A
Yellow-billed Cuckoo *C. americanus*   A

Order STRIGIFORMES
Family TYTONIDAE (barn owls)
Barn Owl *Tyto alba*   A
Family STRIGIDAE (owls)
Scops Owl *Otus scops*   A
Eagle Owl *Bubo bubo*   B
Snowy Owl *Nyctea scandiaca*   A
Hawk Owl *Surnia ulula*   A
Little Owl *Athene noctua*   C
Tawny Owl *Strix aluco*   A
Long-eared Owl *Asio otus*   A
Short-eared Owl *A. flammea*   A
Tengmalm's Owl *Aegolius funereus*   A

Order CAPRIMULGIFORMES
Family CAPRIMULGIDAE (nightjars)
Nightjar *Caprimulgus europaeus*   A
Red-necked Nightjar *C. ruficollis*   B
Egyptian Nightjar *C. aegyptius*   B
Common Nighthawk *Chordeiles minor*   A

Order APODIFORMES
Family APODIDAE (swifts)
Needle-tailed Swift *Hirundapus caudacutus*   A
Swift *Apus apus*   A
Alpine Swift *A. melba*   A
Little Swift *A. affinis*   A

Order CORACIIFORMES
Family ALCEDINIDAE (kingfishers)
Kingfisher *Alcedo atthis*   A
Belted Kingfisher *Ceryle alcyon*   A
Family MEROPIDAE (bee-eaters)
Blue-cheeked Bee-eater *Merops superciliosus*   A
Bee-eater *M. apiaster*   A
Family CORACIIDAE (rollers)
Roller *Coracias garrulus*   A

Order CORACIIFORMES (*cont.*)
    Family UPUPIDAE (hoopoe)
        Hoopoe *Upupa epops* A

Order PICIFORMES
    Family PICIDAE (woodpeckers)
        Wryneck *Jynx torquilla* A
        Yellow-shafted Flicker *Colaptes auratus* D
        Green Woodpecker *Picus viridis* A
        Yellow-bellied Sapsucker *Sphyrapicus varius* A
        Great Spotted Woodpecker *Dendrocopos major* A
        Lesser Spotted Woodpecker *D. minor* A

Order PASSERIFORMES
    Family ALAUDIDAE (larks)
        Calandra Lark *Melanocorypha calandra* A
        Bimaculated Lark *M. bimaculata* A
        White-winged Lark *M. leucoptera* A
        Short-toed Lark *Calandrella brachydactyla* A
        Lesser Short-toed Lark *C. rufescens* A
        Crested Lark *Galerida cristata* A
        Woodlark *Lullula arborea* A
        Skylark *Alauda arvensis* A
        Shore Lark *Eremophila alpestris* A
    Family HIRUNDINIDAE (swallows)
        Sand Martin *Riparia riparia* A
        Swallow *Hirundo rustica* A
        Red-rumped Swallow *H. daurica* A
        House Martin *Delichon urbica* A
    Family MOTACILLIDAE (pipits and wagtails)
        Richard's Pipit *Anthus novaeseelandiae* A
        Blyth's Pipit *A. godlewskii* B
        Tawny Pipit *A. campestris* A
        Olive-backed Pipit *A. hodgsoni* A
        Tree Pipit *A. trivialis* A
        Pechora Pipit *A. gustavi* A
        Meadow Pipit *A. pratensis* A
        Red-throated Pipit *A. cervinus* A
        Rock Pipit *A. spinoletta* A
        Yellow Wagtail *Motacilla flava* A
        Citrine Wagtail *M. citreola* A
        Grey Wagtail *M. cinerea* A
        Pied Wagtail *M. alba* A
    Family BOMBYCILLIDAE (waxwings)
        Waxwing *Bombycilla garrulus* A
    Family CINCLIDAE (dippers)
        Dipper *Cinclus cinclus* A

Family TROGLODYTIDAE (wrens)
Wren *Troglodytes troglodytes*   A
Family MIMIDAE (thrashers)
Brown Thrasher *Toxostoma rufum*   A
Family PRUNELLIDAE (accentors)
Dunnock *Prunella modularis*   A
Alpine Accentor *P. collaris*   A
Family TURDIDAE (thrushes)
Rufous Bush Robin *Cercotrichas galactotes*   A
Robin *Erithacus rubecula*   A
Thrush Nightingale *Luscinia luscinia*   A
Nightingale *L. megarhynchos*   A
Siberian Rubythroat *L. calliope*   A
Bluethroat *L. svecica*   A
Red-flanked Bluetail *Tarsiger cyanurus*   A
Black Redstart *Phoenicurus ochruros*   A
Redstart *P. phoenicurus*   A
Whinchat *Saxicola rubetra*   A
Stonechat *S. torquata*   A
Isabelline Wheatear *Oenanthe isabellina*   B
Wheatear *O. oenanthe*   A
Pied Wheatear *O. pleschanka*   A
Black-eared Wheatear *O. hispanica*   A
Desert Wheatear *O. deserti*   A
Black Wheatear *O. leucura*   A
Rock Thrush *Monticola saxatilis*   A
Blue Rock Thrush *M. solitarius*   D
White's Thrush *Zoothera dauma*   A
Siberian Thrush *Z. sibirica*   A
Hermit Thrush *Catharus guttata*   A
Swainson's Thrush *C. ustulatus*   A
Grey-cheeked Thrush *C. minimus*   A
Veery *C. fuscescens*   A
Ring Ouzel *Turdus torquatus*   A
Blackbird *T. merula*   A
Eye-browed Thrush *T. obscurus*   A
Dusky/Naumann's Thrush *T. naumanni*   A
Black-throated/Red-throated Thrush *T. ruficollis*   A
Fieldfare *T. pilaris*   A
Song Thrush *T. philomelos*   A
Redwing *T. iliacus*   A
Mistle Thrush *T. viscivorus*   A
American Robin *T. migratorius*   A
Family SYLVIIDAE (warblers)
Cetti's Warbler *Cettia cetti*   A
Fan-tailed Warbler *Cisticola juncidis*   A
Pallas's Grasshopper Warbler *Locustella certhiola*   A

Order PASSERIFORMES (cont.)
    Lanceolated Warbler *L. lanceolata*   A
    Grasshopper Warbler *L. naevia*   A
    River Warbler *L. fluviatilis*   A
    Savi's Warbler *L. luscinioides*   A
    Moustached Warbler *Acrocephalus melanopogon*   A
    Aquatic Warbler *A. paludicola*   A
    Sedge Warbler *A. schoenobaenus*   A
    Paddyfield Warbler *A. agricola*   A
    Blyth's Reed Warbler *A. dumetorum*   A
    Marsh Warbler *A. palustris*   A
    Reed Warbler *A. scirpaceus*   A
    Great Reed Warbler *A. arundinaceus*   A
    Thick-billed Warbler *A. aedon*   A
    Olivaceous Warbler *Hippolais pallida*   A
    Booted Warbler *H. caligata*   A
    Icterine Warbler *H. icterina*   A
    Melodious Warbler *H. polyglotta*   A
    Dartford Warbler *Sylvia undata*   A
    Spectacled Warbler *S. conspicillata*   A
    Subalpine Warbler *S. cantillans*   A
    Sardinian Warbler *S. melanocephala*   A
    Rüppell's Warbler *S. rueppelli*   A
    Desert Warbler *S. nana*   A
    Orphean Warbler *S. hortensis*   A
    Barred Warbler *S. nisoria*   A
    Lesser Whitethroat *S. curruca*   A
    Whitethroat *S. communis*   A
    Garden Warbler *S. borin*   A
    Blackcap *S. atricapilla*   A
    Greenish Warbler *Phylloscopus trochiloides*   A
    Arctic Warbler *P. borealis*   A
    Pallas's Warbler *P. proregulus*   A
    Yellow-browed Warbler *P. inornatus*   A
    Radde's Warbler *P. schwarzi*   A
    Dusky Warbler *P. fuscatus*   A
    Bonelli's Warbler *P. bonelli*   A
    Wood Warbler *P. sibilatrix*   A
    Chiffchaff *P. collybita*   A
    Willow Warbler *P. trochilus*   A
    Goldcrest *Regulus regulus*   A
    Firecrest *R. ignicapillus*   A
Family MUSCICAPIDAE (flycatchers)
    Spotted Flycatcher *Muscicapa striata*   A
    Red-breasted Flycatcher *Ficedula parva*   A
    Collared Flycatcher *F. albicollis*   A
    Pied Flycatcher *F. hypoleuca*   A

Family TIMALIIDAE (babblers)
    Bearded Tit *Panurus biarmicus*   A
Family AEGITHALIDAE (long-tailed tits)
    Long-tailed Tit *Aegithalos caudatus*   A
Family PARIDAE (tits)
    Marsh Tit *Parus palustris*   A
    Willow Tit *P. montanus*   A
    Crested Tit *P. cristatus*   A
    Coal Tit *P. ater*   A
    Blue Tit *P. caeruleus*   A
    Great Tit *P. major*   A
Family SITTIDAE (nuthatches)
    Nuthatch *Sitta europaea*   A
Family TICHODROMADIDAE (wallcreeper)
    Wallcreeper *Tichodroma muraria*   A
Family CERTHIIDAE (treecreepers)
    Treecreeper *Certhia familiaris*   A
    Short-toed Treecreeper *C. brachydactyla*   A
Family REMIZIDAE (penduline tits)
    Penduline Tit *Remiz pendulinus*   A
Family ORIOLIDAE (orioles)
    Golden Oriole *Oriolus oriolus*   A
Family LANIIDAE (shrikes)
    Isabelline Shrike *Lanius isabellinus*   A
    Red-backed Shrike *L. collurio*   A
    Lesser Grey Shrike *L. minor*   A
    Great Grey Shrike *L. excubitor*   A
    Woodchat Shrike *L. senator*   A
Family CORVIDAE (crows)
    Jay *Garrulus glandarius*   A
    Magpie *Pica pica*   A
    Nutcracker *Nucifraga caryocatactes*   A
    Chough *Pyrrhocorax pyrrhocorax*   A
    Jackdaw *Corvus monedula*   A
    Rook *C. frugilegus*   A
    Carrion Crow *C. corone*   A
    Raven *C. corax*   A
Family STURNIDAE (starlings)
    Starling *Sturnus vulgaris*   A
    Rose-coloured Starling *S. roseus*   A
Family PASSERIDAE (sparrows)
    House Sparrow *Passer domesticus*   A
    Spanish Sparrow *P. hispaniolensis*   A
    Tree Sparrow *P. montanus*   A
Family VIREONIDAE (vireos)
    Red-eyed Vireo *Vireo olivaceus*   A

Order PASSERIFORMES (*cont.*)
  Family FRINGILLIDAE (finches)
    Chaffinch *Fringilla coelebs*   A
    Brambling *F. montifringilla*   A
    Serin *Serinus serinus*   A
    Citril Finch *S. citrinella*   B
    Greenfinch *Carduelis chloris*   A
    Goldfinch *C. carduelis*   A
    Siskin *C. spinus*   A
    Linnet *C. cannabina*   A
    Twite *C. flavirostris*   A
    Redpoll *C. flammea*   A
    Arctic Redpoll *C. hornemanni*   A
    Two-barred Crossbill *Loxia leucoptera*   A
    Crossbill *L. curvirostra*   A
    Scottish Crossbill *L. scotica*   A
    Parrot Crossbill *L. pytyopsittacus*   A
    Trumpeter Finch *Bucanetes githagineus*   A
    Scarlet Rosefinch *Carpodacus erythrinus*   A
    Pine Grosbeak *Pinicola enucleator*   A
    Bullfinch *Pyrrhula pyrrhula*   A
    Hawfinch *Coccothraustes coccothraustes*   A
    Evening Grosbeak *Hesperiphona vespertina*   A
  Family PARULIDAE (New World warblers)
    Black-and-White Warbler *Mniotilta varia*   A
    Tennessee Warbler *Vermivora peregrina*   A
    Parula Warbler *Parula americana*   A
    Yellow Warbler *Dendroica petechia*   A
    Cape May Warbler *D. tigrina*   A
    Yellow-rumped Warbler *D. coronata*   A
    Palm Warbler *D. palmarum*   D
    Blackpoll Warbler *D. striata*   A
    American Redstart *Setophaga ruticilla*   A
    Ovenbird *Seiurus aurocapillus*   A
    Northern Waterthrush *S. noveboracensis*   A
    Yellowthroat *Geothlypis trichas*   A
    Hooded Warbler *Wilsonia citrina*   A
  Family THRAUPIDAE (tanagers)
    Summer Tanager *Piranga rubra*   A
    Scarlet Tanager *P. olivacea*   A
  Family EMBERIZIDAE (buntings and New World sparrows)
    Rufous-sided Towhee *Pipilo erythrophthalmus*   A
    Fox Sparrow *Zonotrichia iliaca*   A
    Song Sparrow *Z. melodia*   A
    White-crowned Sparrow *Z. leucophrys*   A
    White-throated Sparrow *Z. albicollis*   A
    Slate-coloured Junco *Junco hyemalis*   A

Lapland Bunting *Calcarius lapponicus*   A
Snow Bunting *Plectrophenax nivalis*   A
Pine Bunting *Emberiza leucocephalos*   A
Yellowhammer *E. citrinella*   A
Cirl Bunting *E. cirlus*   A
Rock Bunting *E. cia*   A
Ortolan Bunting *E. hortulana*   A
Cretzschmar's Bunting *E. caesia*   A
Rustic Bunting *E. rustica*   A
Little Bunting *E. pusilla*   A
Chestnut Bunting *E. rutila*   D
Yellow-breasted Bunting *E. aureola*   A
Reed Bunting *E. schoeniclus*   A
Pallas's Reed Bunting *E. pallasi*   A
Red-headed Bunting *E. bruniceps*   D
Black-headed Bunting *E. melanocephala*   A
Corn Bunting *Miliaria calandra*   A
Rose-breasted Grosbeak *Pheucticus ludovicianus*   A
Blue Grosbeak *Guiraca caerulea*   D
Indigo Bunting *Passerina cyanea*   D
Painted Bunting *P. ciris*   D
Family ICTERIDAE (New World blackbirds)
Bobolink *Dolichonyx oryzivorus*   A
Northern Oriole *Icterus galbula*   A